PRAISE FOR #FUTUREGEN

'Be inspired by this fascinating story of how Wales made into law the obligation for a country to pursue sustainable development on behalf of future generations.'

GRO HARLEM BRUNDTLAND, former Prime Minister of Norway and Director-General of the World Health Organization

'The very definition of sustainable development embodies the need to ensure the well-being of future generations and yet, until Wales in 2015 enacted its Well-being of Future Generations Act, no country had passed legislation to look ahead and give itself the ambition, permission and legal obligation to improve social, cultural, environmental and economic dimensions of well-being for current and future generations. Jane Davidson was a pioneer in pushing forward Wales's pathbreaking Future Generations Act, blazing a trail for the rest of the world, and WWF was delighted and honoured to support her on that journey. Decision-makers everywhere should read her book to understand the importance of putting future generations at the heart of all they do and the actions needed to make that a reality.'

PAVAN SUKHDEV, President, WWF International

'A truly pioneering Act that puts sustainability at the heart of every governmental decision combined with a country seeking to reimagine itself – the story of this revolutionary engine for change holds enormous possibility and is a true beacon of hope.'

MICHAEL SHEEN OBE, actor and UNICEF ambassador

'As the effects of climate change and ecological degradation become ever more apparent it is not despair that must drive us, but action. Jane Davidson's wonderful #futuregen tells the inspiring story of how one country stepped up with just that – a groundbreaking new law to protect the interests of future generations. For those searching for hope, this is a must-read.'

TONY JUNIPER CBE, Environmentalist

'Once at the forefront of the industrial revolution, Wales now leads the world in the sustainability revolution. At the intersection of sustainability, economics, law, morality and politics, the Well-being of Future Generations (Wales) Act enshrines the responsibility of a government to take care of its citizens, especially the vulnerable, and extends that responsibility to those who are the most vulnerable because they do not yet have a voice – the generations as yet unborn. In #*futuregen*, Jane Davidson, its chief architect, relates what inspired this groundbreaking Act and what impact it has had in the five years since it was passed. Politicians are not generally noted for their long-term, upstream thinking. Influenced by systems thinker Donella Meadows, Jane Davidson is an inspiring exception and has earned the gratitude of generations both future and current.'

ROZ SAVAGE MBE, ocean rower and sustainability advocate

'Please give this book to the sons and daughters of our leaders, then ask them to give it to their parents. Maybe they won't make the change needed for the people who voted them in, but they might just do it for their children.'

DAVID HIEATT, co-founder, Hiut Denim Co.
and The Do Lectures; author

#futuregen

#futuregen

Lessons *from a* Small Country

JANE DAVIDSON

Chelsea Green Publishing
White River Junction, Vermont
London, UK

Project Manager: Sarah Kovach
Project Editor: Jon Rae
Developmental Editor: Muna Reyal
Copy Editor: Laura Jorstad
Proofreader: Angela Boyle
Indexer: Nancy Crompton
Designer: Melissa Jacobson

Printed in the United States of America.
First printing May 2020.
10 9 8 7 6 5 4 3 2   20 21 22 23 24

Library of Congress Cataloging-in-Publication Data
Names: Davidson, Jane, 1957– author.
Title: #FutureGen : lessons from a small country / Jane Davidson.
Description: White River Junction, Vermont : Chelsea Green Publishing, [2020]
  | Includes bibliographical references and index.
Identifiers: LCCN 2020011134 (print) | LCCN 2020011135 (ebook) |
  ISBN 9781603589604 (hardcover) | ISBN 9781603589611 (ebook)
  | ISBN 9781603589628 (audio)
Subjects: LCSH: Wales. Wellbeing of Future Generations Act. | Sustainable
  development—Government policy—Wales. | Sustainable development—Law
  and legislation—Wales. | Public policy (Law)—Wales. | Wales—Social policy.
Classification: LCC HV249.W354 D37 2020 (print) | LCC HV249.W354 (ebook)
  | DDC 344.42904/6—dc23
LC record available at https://lccn.loc.gov/2020011134
LC ebook record available at https://lccn.loc.gov/2020011135

Chelsea Green Publishing
85 North Main Street, Suite 120
White River Junction, Vermont USA

Somerset House
London, UK

www.chelseagreen.com

DEDICATION

This book is dedicated posthumously to

Rhodri Morgan, whom I first met in 1983 as the Labour candidate for the parliamentary seat of Cardiff West. Rhodri was a man both charismatic and kind; for whom I worked in his constituency office and in Parliament for five years; with whom I bicycled and walked and laughed and debated. He helped forge my conviction politics; he brought me into his first cabinet in 2000 when he became First Minister of Wales; and he always believed in me and trusted me to deliver law and policy for current and future generations.

Morgan Parry, whom I met in 2007, then director of WWF in Wales, a gentle advocate with steely resolve; even more delighted by my new responsibilities as Minister for Environment, Sustainability and Housing than I was and determined to help me make the most of the opportunity. Morgan's influence on me was profound because he lived his values and taught me to do the same. He worried about his and Wales' carbon footprint, acted accordingly and challenged the rest of us to act commensurately.

Both were cruelly wrenched from their families before their time, but their influence lives on. Without either of them there would be no story to tell.

CONTENTS

Introduction: For Our Future Generations   1

1 **From Nature to Politics:**
How They Became One   9

2 **Visioning:** The Journey to the Act, 1992–2011   25

3 **Networking:** The Act and Its Delivery
in Wales, 2011–2015   69

4 **Truth-telling:** Keeping the Pressure
on the Act and Its Ambition   103

5 **Learning:** Living the Spirit of the Act   137

6 **Loving:** Wild Ideas for Wales and
the Wider World   155

Endnote: My Journey to Living Lightly   171

The Last Word by Sophie Howe, Wales' first Future
Generations Commissioner   175

Acknowledgements   179

Appendix 1: 'One Wales, One Planet':
Our Vision of Sustainable Wales   181

Appendix 2: Useful Resources   187

Index   195

'Our inherent short-termism and [the] inability of individuals to act effectively for the future on their own is why legislation to reflect future generations' interests is required in all countries.'

Tony Juniper, CBE, environmentalist

'We the citizenry through our elected members have allowed the existence of corporations of limited liability to come into being without any effective way of auditing the impact of corporations on the common . . . wealth. Were every corporation to have to give one golden share to the people via their government, which came with the obligation on its auditors to measure every possible impact on that common resource, we would have few environmental problems today as purpose and ethics would have triumphed over greed unmastered and the moral compass could be reset.

'Some of my friends tell me I'm a dreamer, but I'm not the only one . . . join us!'

Tim Smit, founder, Eden Project, Cornwall

'The glory of the Welsh Act is that it was never just a law. It is the essence of culture. It glows through the social bloodstream of the nation, energising and recreating itself through the pores of everyday life.'

Tim O'Riordan, Emeritus Professor, School of Environmental Sciences, University of East Anglia, and Fellow of the British Academy

Introduction

For Our Future Generations

*The eyes of all future generations are upon you.
And if you choose to fail us, I say we will never forgive you*

GRETA THUNBERG, 2019 UN Climate Action Summit

*We hope that what Wales does today, the world will do
tomorrow. Action, more than words, is the hope for our
current and future generations.*

NIKHIL SETH, head of sustainable development,
United Nations Development Programme

In 2015 our government in Wales passed into law the Well-being of Future Generations (Wales) Act. This Act is the first legislation in the world to enshrine the rights of future generations alongside current ones and requires Welsh Government ministers and the organisations they oversee to embed this commitment into everything they do.

When it received Royal Assent in 2015, Carl Sargeant AM (Assembly Member), the sponsoring minister, said: 'By passing the Well-being of Future Generations Act, we have formally placed sustainable development at the heart of our public services and legislated for a set of goals – linked to the UN's Global Goals – that set a clear path to a sustainable future.'

The creation of the Act was a brave and wonderful deed by the Welsh Government and a vote of confidence by the Welsh legislature for a different, more sustainable future for Wales. The Act proposes simply that the effect of decisions on the needs of future generations is factored into the decision-making process and gives guidance on how to do that – it provides permission to think sustainably in an unsustainable world. It is revolutionary because it enshrines into law that the well-being of the current and future people of Wales is explicitly the core purpose of the government of Wales – the principle at the heart of government.

Such a core principle is revolutionary in its own right, but the Act goes further: after specifying the intention, it shows us how to get there – becoming a framework for collective action. If you ask the question, 'What does the Act do?', it creates seven goals for living within our environmental limits in the arenas of health, prosperity, resilience, communities, language and heritage, equality and Wales' role in the world.

If you ask the question, 'How should people comply with the Act?', it directs five ways of working to reach decisions: prevention, long-termism, collaboration, participation and integrating activities to reach positive outcomes for as many of the goals as possible. The seven goals are the *what*; the five ways of working are the *how*. This is a moral agenda, predicated not on what is right in the short term or for individual benefit, but on what is right for the well-being of our communities, our countries and our very existence as humans in nature.

I write this story as the minister who proposed the Act. I recount what led up to it, examine why Wales was first to do it and then assess whether it is working and what needs to happen next. Many times I have been asked about why I wanted to create a law to benefit future generations. I didn't set out to do that, but when I asked myself how we could reset the needle for a new age of politics and offer hope to future generations and to nature – which doesn't have a vote – I came to the conclusion that the only way to ensure a positive future for the next generation, and the ones that follow, is for government to act differently now. I've been called its mother, its architect, its creator, all of which are very flattering, but not accurate. I accept that if I had not been in the ministerial position that I was, at the time that I was, we may not have an act in Wales now, but this is probably more to do with my inherent obstinacy, a refusal to take no for an answer on something I believe in, than any higher motive.

This book is a frank account of the journey Wales took from my personal perspective, hopefully answering the questions 'why Wales?' and 'why now?', along with looking at whether the first country in the world to take legislative action specifically to protect generations yet to come is doing the job envisaged.

Lessons from a small country

The story of Wales is a story of ambition. In 1999 this small country sought a new opportunity, through its new legislature, the National Assembly for Wales, to reframe the traditional role of government by creating a new context in which to inspire better decisions in the interests of current and future generations.

People of Wales have big hearts. They belong in a small country, but, oh man, they really have the kick of a mule!
ARCHBISHOP DESMOND TUTU

I am strongly of the belief that there are particular opportunities for a small country to be a test bed; to be smarter and more flexible than its larger neighbours. Here cultural behaviour-change experiments can be piloted and new approaches forged.

Culturally, Wales has sustained the oldest Celtic language in the world into current use. The Welsh language has official status in Wales, and all political parties are encouraging its expansion. Many people who come to Wales for the first time are surprised to hear that a fifth of people in Wales speak Welsh as their first language as they go about their daily activities. Nearly a third of school pupils receive all or most of their education in Welsh. I live in one of the many places in Wales where all services are naturally delivered in Welsh by Welsh speakers. This makes it a very different environment to other parts of the U.K. and is worthy of celebration. The National Eisteddfod of Wales, which dates back to Cardigan Castle in 1176, is not only the annual celebration of Welsh language and culture and the largest celebration of minority-language culture in Europe but is also the largest poetry and music festival in Europe, recognised globally by its ancient Red Dragon flag that is proudly outside the Union Jack. Its young person equivalent, the Urdd National Eisteddfod – the annual Welsh-language youth festival of literature, music and the performing arts – is also Europe's largest youth festival. I will come back later to the important part Welsh language and culture play in the Well-being of Future Generations Act.

Wales is both a nation with an ancient parliamentary history going back to 1404 and a modern vibrant country with world-class universities and fantastic natural resources – its coasts and its mountains bring tourists from all over the world. Many people who come to university here never leave because of the quality of the natural environment. Adjacent to its second city, Swansea, lies the Gower Peninsula, the first designated Area of Outstanding Natural Beauty in the U.K. The Gower's beaches have regularly featured among the best in the U.K., as have those in the county I live in, Pembrokeshire, and the Llŷn Peninsula and the island of Anglesey in North Wales. Snowdonia, the mountainous region in the north, is famed for hosting the second highest mountain in the U.K. and the world's steepest road.

But Wales' beauty and its modern, outward-looking approach bely a darker legacy.

Wales is often recognised as the first industrial country, whose considerable wealth and health was extracted from it for the benefit of people elsewhere. Wales has often led innovation. The 1841 census showed it to be the first country in history to move from agriculture to industry; the first £1 million cheque ever was signed here, in the Cardiff Coal Exchange. Its industrial development, while kick-starting the industrial revolution, was based primarily on coal, iron, copper and steel and came at an appalling cost to both its environment and the health and well-being of its people. Quarrying was the other key

Introduction

industry that fuelled the revolution, with stone used for buildings and roads. Records and pictures from the 19th century are accounts of hell, where the work was impossibly hard, conducted in atmospheres of belching smoke, dangerous blasting, poisonous fumes or the unstable dark of the mines. As we leave the old industries behind, there is a danger that we also leave behind the current and future generations of the thousands of families who contributed to Wales' industrial strength.

With this industrial heritage, Wales unsurprisingly has a very poor health record, with life expectancies varying by five years. Inequalities in health are most pronounced in areas that also experienced social and economic deprivation, such as South Wales' former mining valleys.

Wales has a small population – fewer than 4 million – with substantial cultural diversity in the towns and cities with docks, where different communities have integrated well for over a century. The Labour Party has been the dominant political force in Wales for more than a century. Social justice and tackling poverty remain key political themes, as does a wider equality agenda including ethnicity and gender. There is a pervading feeling in communities 'left behind' by the move away from coal and steel – and with some justification – that they did all the work and did not receive the benefit. If any country needs to look after the health and well-being of future generations, it is Wales!

But how resilient is it as a nation? According to Professor Herbert Girardet of the World Future Council, the South Wales valleys are surrounded by hills rich in wind-, solar- and hydro-power potential. Surprisingly, he says, very little of this has so far been developed – and hardly any to the benefit of local communities:

In Wales, so far, some £2 billion has been invested in onshore and offshore wind turbines, generating over £340 million in revenue per annum, largely to the benefit of remote shareholders. Not surprisingly, in the Valleys there has been strong resistance against new wind power development. Why should the intrusion of large wind farms into the local countryside be tolerated if it has few tangible benefits to local people? But whilst large-scale wind, hydro and solar energy development cannot replace the 100,000 former coal and steel industry jobs in the Valleys, it could, nevertheless, spawn many new businesses and job opportunities, and a huge revenue stream for local communities.

For years the notion of getting on in Wales was to get out – and indeed the 20th century saw Welsh emigration across the world. In this century, however, there are signs of people wanting to come back to Wales, citing quality of life, distinctiveness, the Welsh language and increasingly the fact that Wales now has its own legislature. Excitingly, the Well-being of Future Generations (Wales) Act itself is becoming a tool of Wales' 'soft power' in the world, where its very existence tells you about the characteristics of a nation open to change and prepared to be responsible for future generations.

We live in interesting times. We might be the poorest country in the U.K., but we are innovators: at the forefront of genetic and Alzheimer's disease research, but also the world's first Fairtrade nation, a world leader in recycling, a U.K. leader in organ donation, one of the only countries in the world where 'you can walk the shape of a nation' along our coast and of course the first country in the world to legislate for future generations.

In so many ways, it would be easy to suggest that we live in very dark times: when drawbridges are being pulled up across the world; when those fleeing persecution, famine, disease or flood are turned back at borders, sometimes losing their lives in the process. But there is hope – hope from individuals, from movements, from science, from politics. One of my favourite calls to action is often attributed to Margaret Mead, the anthropologist: 'Never doubt that a small group of thoughtful, committed citizens can change the world; indeed, it is the only thing that ever has.'

We have been and are being transformative, we have been and are used to big ambition; but making this huge commitment to living

Introduction

more sustainably for the benefit of current and future generations –
how exciting and groundbreaking is that? If lessons from the small
country of Wales can help keep the intergenerational beacon alight,
my job will have been well done.

During my years in government and more recently in the writing
of this book, I spoke and corresponded extensively with the people
mentioned in these pages, and these conversations were the source for
their words here, including the quotes that open each chapter. Links
to the statutory Sustainable Development Schemes and Effectiveness
Reviews discussed here can be found in the useful resources on page
187, together with links to other useful or relevant reports

'What is so compelling about the "future generations" approach is the way it gives governments and decision-makers worldwide a tangible, almost personal reason to act and think long-term. Thinking of fairness, justice, equity – however you choose to frame it – in terms of the interests and well-being of our own children, grandchildren and great-grandchildren makes the demands of future generations suddenly more urgent and more immediate.'

Catarina Tully, director, School of International Futures

'The Well-being of Future Generations Act represents a part of our society that cannot stand up for itself yet. Enshrined in its remit is to protect the future. Let's hope it does that and is able to create its own form of immortality by reproducing itself.'

Juliet Davenport, founder and CEO, Good Energy

CHAPTER 1

From Nature to Politics

How They Became One

We can never have enough of Nature.

HENRY DAVID THOREAU

I remember the moment I fell in love with the abundance of nature. It was 1964 and I was seven years old, newly kitted out with my birthday bicycle, a glorious translucent red BSA (Birmingham Small Arms) steel creation which was my winged chariot, my explorer's horse. On it I would cycle to school and, much more important, was allowed to go on my own across wasteland and veldt in the unfinished suburb of Mount Pleasant in Salisbury, Rhodesia. In that year of the bicycle, snakes crossed my path, as did monkeys, the occasional herd of duiker or Thomson's gazelle and an enormous variety of insects and spiders of fantastic sizes and colours. My favourite were the chongololos, wonderfully armoured millipedes, bigger than my hands, which at the first sign of danger would curl up into tightly wrought shiny golden circles, paired legs curled beautifully in order. As a child, I spent hours encouraging as many chongololos as possible to be rings on my fingers – until they fell off when, in their view, danger was averted. I remember 26 being my goal – 3 on each of my longer fingers and 2 each on the little finger and thumb – but I don't remember ever achieving anything like that. Chongololos get bored easily, as it turns out.

I remember the trees in my life – the custard apple outside our back door; the rustling murmur of our neighbour's tall eucalyptuses outside my bedroom window with their silvery bark and sharp tang when licked; the stately *Acrocarpus* (pink cedar) towering above the drive – which I was forbidden to climb, but had such delectable horizontal branches, rising ladderlike into the skies. There were the fruit trees rich with their citrus aromas, particularly the naartje – a native version of a tangerine, twice the size and a hundred times the flavour; the avocado pears and mangoes growing wild wherever their seeds had landed. Not forgetting the baobab – once witnessed, never forgotten – the upside-down tree, looking for all the world as if it were waving its roots in the air. More than any other plant, the baobab captured my childhood imagination. To this day a picture of one brings memories of my childhood in Africa flooding back: the smell of red earth after rain in the wet season, azure skies with endless promise of picnics and exploring and swimming in the dry season and a cacophony of sounds and colours assaulting the senses; nature in harmony and on display, infiltrating all my senses, abundant and ever giving. I was part of nature and nature was part of me. Together we were whole.

Unbeknownst to me at the time, this is when the wildness of nature entered my soul and became an essential part of who I was then and who I am now: not the tidy, regimented planting of suburban gardens (although I'm always impressed at the effort involved) but geology and animals in their natural habitats – the lushness of tiny ferns making dead trees their home; the joy of the swallows' nests in the eaves of the garage; the nest of slow worms in the compost heap; the majesty of mountains and what their existence does to the sky above; the plunging, bent, tortured geology of the coastal cliffs; the flick of a dolphin's tail; the plaintive call of an oystercatcher; the feel of the bark of a tree; the scent of spring. I am the one hand clapping in the forest, leaving behind only footprints. These treasures are there for us all, every single day of our lives if we look – and they need protecting. I've started each chapter therefore with a reflection on what nature speaks to me and how that integrates with my thinking about the opportunities from the Well-being of Future Generations Act for Wales and elsewhere.

Early upbringing

I was brought up in Zimbabwe when it was called Rhodesia. My professor father had been seconded by the University of Birmingham in 1962 to establish a new multiracial medical school at the University College of Rhodesia in its capital, Salisbury (now Harare). The medical school was to be a beacon of hope in southern Africa, training indigenous doctors of all colours and creeds.

Both my parents had strong notions of fairness and service. My mother, also a doctor, worked for the Rhodesian Family Planning Service on a part-time basis, often in remote parts of the country. I grew up with three household staff – a cook (Godfrey), a nanny (Mary), both of whom were effectively family, and with us all through my early life, and a succession of gardeners. We lived in a house with a veranda in a quiet professional district close to the university. The staff lived in a kia (a small, rather Spartan brick house) at the bottom of our garden, and we were required to treat them all with respect. Everyone's childhood is unique in the sense it is the prism though which their lives are lived. My childhood was idyllic with its abundance of nature and freedom.

Three incidents over a period of years penetrated my idyll enough to start me seeing the worm in my Eden, the racism underpinning the right-wing Rhodesian Front government after the United Declaration of Independence from the U.K. in 1965. The first was in relation to our next-door neighbours. We had moved into a newly built bungalow on a large plot – still with its ancient msasa (zebra tree) redolent of the previous veldt – in a developing professional suburb close to the university. Next door was a similar-sized plot. Prior to the sale, the builder checked with my parents that they were happy living next door to a 'coloured' family. They were, and we lived comfortably side by side for years until they were summarily removed as Mount Pleasant, where we lived, had been designated a 'whites only' district. The second was going round to a new school friend's home for tea and watching with horror her family's verbal and physical abuse of their house staff. That was the end of our incipient friendship and another wake-up call in my Eden. The third was when I was with my nanny Mary, whom I loved dearly, at a park in the centre of Salisbury. She ushered me through the gate into the park we'd been in together many times before, but now she had to stay on the other side of the new notice that said, 'Whites Only'.

I don't know what it takes as a child to understand that what you are witnessing is wrong, but I know that the combination of the summary removal, physical and verbal abuse and forced separation on the basis of colour and race made me realise not only that the values of the society I was living in were very wrong but that I could never endorse such behaviour. I was seven when I had my first epiphany about fairness, but it was rooted in my parents' upbringing of fairness and respect for all humans, irrespective of race, culture or creed, which has been at the heart of my own values ever since.

When I was 14, my father decided to return to the U.K. to go back into clinical practice, and I was parcelled up and sent to a boarding school in middle England, some nine months ahead of the family move. It was sophisticated and wealthy; I was awkward, naive, resentful. I was African. I didn't want to live in the U.K. I hated being caged in the school and would break out regularly to walk – often on my own – on the neighbouring hills, sitting watching nesting birds, hunting for adders or swimming in the quarry – I contravened every regulation possible. It took me years to find my place in that school, but what never left me was that extraordinary culture shock of consumerism when I arrived; guilty parents compensating for their absence by increasingly enormous amounts of 'stuff'. I was too young to reject it confidently then, but growing up under sanctions in a country where nothing was wasted was a hugely formative experience, building in me a hatred of waste and particularly of a throwaway culture, which led to my later passion for a zero-waste agenda for Wales.

One abiding immensely positive memory of my school experience, which ultimately led to the creation of the Wales Coast Path, was spending a fortnight walking the new Pembrokeshire Coast Path with school friends. On this, one of the first National Trails in the U.K., we saw dolphins, porpoises and seabirds galore, including Manx shearwaters and puffins on a boat visit to the island of Skomer. One indelible image was of arriving towards sunset at the youth hostel at Pwll Deri, close to Strumble Head, which is perched on high, vertical cliffs looking westward out to sea and southward to the Pembrokeshire coast back to St David's Head. There, in the middle of the deep pool below the hostel, was a huge Portuguese man o' war, with a bright blue float above a pink body and long tentacles splayed around it in the setting sun. Unforgettable.

I studied English literature at university and, as part of the course, had taken a module on American literature. *Walden; or, Life in the Woods*, written by Henry David Thoreau in 1854, details his experiences over the course of 26 months in a cabin he built in woodland owned by friend and mentor Ralph Waldo Emerson. I had been out very late the previous night and had not read the book. In class I kept my head down both physically and metaphorically. The rain was lashing against the windows, and small drops of water were puddling gently and rhythmically on the windowsill. The sonorous voice of the lecturer dripped into my consciousness, comparing the importance of closeness to nature with the 'desperate' existence that Thoreau argues is the lot of most people. Simplicity was his model; make do and mend, minimising consumer activity; become self-reliant. He emphasised the importance of solitude and contemplation. In my dazed state, I was hooked. I loved the metaphor of four seasons symbolising human development and the author's encouragement for people to acquire the four necessities of life (food, shelter, clothing and fuel) to then focus their efforts on personal growth. An early iteration perhaps of the idea that was to be represented by Maslow's hierarchy of needs in 1943, with physiological needs (food, water, shelter, clothing, rest) at the base of the pyramid and self-actualisation (achieving one's full potential) at the top.

As a young teacher, I lived where I do now in north Pembrokeshire, a 'hippie smallholders' destination since John Seymour moved here in 1964. Seymour was the self-sufficiency guru whose seminal books remain relevant now – a man ahead of his time. All my friends who had come here in the 1970s were trying to live lightly on the land, and the school was filled with their children. We gardened, foraged, baked and brewed, swam and walked and cycled; no one had much money, but the warmth of the community was second to none. This experience was the genesis of an idea that later became One Planet Developments to help young people in particular to buy agricultural land affordably in exchange for living very low-carbon lives.

Apprenticeships: politics and policy

I think many people become activists by discovering that they are no longer prepared to tolerate particular actions. The move from 'someone should do or say something' to doing it or saying it yourself may take a long time, but I certainly know that my generation, particularly women, became galvanised into resistance politics as a response to Margaret Thatcher's leadership. In 1983 I moved to my second school in Pontypridd – which I later represented in the National Assembly of Wales. This was an important year of political awakening for me, coming to work in the South Wales valleys at a time in which the Thatcher government was at loggerheads with teachers and also with miners – culminating in the year-long miners' strike in 1984, which affected many of our pupils. I became a part-time youth worker just when the Thatcher government reduced its support for youth work. I decided to join a political party – I was ready: honed by my membership in a teaching union, angry at the Tory government's casual indifference to the next generation.

I went to the library to read the party manifestos for the coming general election. I started with the Labour Party as many of my teacher colleagues were members and was immediately wooed and won by the Labour Party manifesto, 'The New Hope for Britain', drawn up under the leadership of Michael Foot. The manifesto filled me with hope and optimism – here was a party whose members believed in creating policies and laws to improve women's rights, tackle racial discrimination, improve education and health for all, look after the most vulnerable in society, create more open government, tackle pollution and lead nuclear disarmament. I'm still a strong supporter of all such initiatives now.

Four years later I was a local councillor in the inner-city community of Riverside in Cardiff where I lived, a stone's throw from the city centre, a community of 29 languages and traditional inner-city problems particularly linked to the private rented housing sector. My fellow councillors at the time were Sue Essex, Jane Hutt and Mark Drakeford (the current First Minister of Wales). Together, we all went on to become Assembly Members, to be in the Welsh cabinet and have the responsibility for embedding sustainable development in the National Assembly – of which more anon. I want to pay them and Rhodri Morgan, the former First Minister, an enormous tribute: they were all conviction politicians rather than career politicians. None of them has ever put their careers before their principles, which for me is a fundamental position.

Effectively, this was my decade of political apprenticeship. I was developing an understanding of the interaction between politics and social policy, and it was exciting also to work with local councillor colleagues to set up such initiatives such as a workplace nursery and a housing help centre in Cardiff. Then came the opportunity to work for Rhodri Morgan, who would become such a huge influence on my life.

Working with Rhodri and my Riverside colleagues was a campaigning apprenticeship accompanied by conviction and humour. We tackled the key issues together, whether that was access to services, tackling the inequalities in the private rented sector, creating childcare opportunities, fighting the poll tax – where I lost my party whip temporarily by refusing to support it – or joining forces with the Royal Society for the Protection of Birds (RSPB) to campaign against the proposed Cardiff Bay Barrage on environmental and social justice grounds. Although we lost that last campaign, we did win considerable concessions to benefit our constituents, and it was an object lesson in using good-quality evidence to change minds. For four years

#futuregen

I undertook the casework and research for Rhodri, who was later the face of popularising Welsh devolution and who would become my mentor, leader and friend. I divided my time working for him between the Cardiff office and the House of Commons and so learned about parliamentary procedures as well as constituency work.

Through much of my constituency and research work for Rhodri and as a local councillor, I was gaining a real picture of the lives of our constituents – and they were often grim. We did not have food banks in those days, but churches in particular were supporting people who were struggling between heating and eating; the majority of our cases were linked to poorly timed benefit payments and poor-quality housing, and there was totally inadequate support for children or adults with special needs. Schools were worried that children were coming in poorly fed and clothed; absenteeism and disruption were rising. Youth clubs were closing through lack of funds. The Joseph Rowntree Foundation has published poverty data over 40 years, and we received the updates in the constituency office. The picture of the U.K.'s – and in particular Wales'– continuing slide into poverty and inequality was terrifying. In the early 1990s nearly a third of all Welsh families lived in poverty, and that doubled for lone parents. No wonder we had queues of desperate people at our surgeries.

I started to focus on social policy research to address poverty and found that across Wales only a few local authorities had anti-poverty action plans, despite the statistics, although under Sue Essex's leadership, Cardiff City Council was one of them. In early 1993 a new National Local Government Forum Against Poverty was looking for five coordinators across the U.K., including one in Wales. Although it was a real wrench leaving Rhodri's office, this was a huge opportunity for me to work with councils of all political persuasions to focus on tackling this critical issue.

With new local authorities came a new pan-Wales organisation, the Welsh Local Government Association, which was looking for staff to lead policy representation from the new Welsh councils to the bodies that could affect the interests of Wales. I became its first Head of Social

Affairs, a perfect brief for me that included health, housing and social services. The three years working in this environment, dealing with local government officials, civil servants and politicians of all parties, prior to the National Assembly starting in 1999, were invaluable to me in understanding how public services worked and their interface with all levels of government.

What motivates me

It would be wonderful to say that I emerged fully formed as a dedicated campaigner for a more sustainable future from my early childhood. But that was not the case. What would be true to say is that my own experience has always influenced the actions I wanted to take as a politician! Time and again in this book, I will emphasise the importance of personal experience as a driver of action. We are all campaigners in our souls! Think for a moment about what motivates you in your own life. I became a local councillor because I felt that 'something must be done'. In my role as a young mother, juggling childcare needs for three young children with work, I recognised the difficulties that working parents had with childcare, so, along with others, I campaigned successfully to establish a workplace nursery. Similarly, as a local councillor in an inner-city ward with poor housing conditions, I witnessed a housing crisis, particularly in the private rented sector, so we set up a housing help centre for people with housing difficulties to gain advice and support.

When I'm not working, I'm probably walking, picking up litter on the way. So for me as a walker, being given the chance later in life to create the Wales Coast Path was an absolute dream. Last year I finished walking the 'the shape of the nation' of Wales, including the beautiful Offa's Dyke upland and inland path down the spine between England and Wales. What a journey – an industrial, natural journey of the history, society, nature and geography of today's Wales. A journey that the creation of the longest circular walking opportunity in the U.K. has given to all, connecting the coast with its adjacent communities.

Unlike many other countries, the coastline of Wales is mostly accessible to the public rather than serving as expensive real estate.

A hater of single-use plastic, I'm particularly proud that we were first in the U.K. to put a charge on carrier bags – a proposal that came from a member of the public. I was determined that we in the Welsh Government would lead action on this. Just think of the satisfaction that I now feel, 11 years on, that the statutory municipal recycling targets we introduced in 2009 (with hefty financial penalties) now mean that Wales is up with the very best in the world.

As a smallholder with stewardship responsibility for two fields and a woodland, growing as much of our own food as we can, I am acutely aware that those who never see the countryside, who experience food in plastic wrappings, separated from its origin, need to be reconnected to that land as the absolute foundation of human survival and well-being. Making this opportunity available to others through One Planet Developments, which is helping young people in particular to buy land for low-impact development that is zero-carbon in construction and use, is for me a way of offering apprenticeships in sustainable living.

I started my working life as a teacher so, when given the opportunity as Minister of Education to reform the curriculum and make it more relevant, I seized it. My early piloting of a new curriculum for three-to-seven-year-olds, based on areas of learning rather than subjects, is the basis of the new Welsh statutory curriculum for all ages by 2022.

The motivation for all of this stemmed from particular passions, people, times and places. Our formative experiences drive our actions, and that became my approach to policy making. If you feel that your own life, as well as other people's, can become fairer by an action you take – then you are super motivated to do it.

It was much later that I realised that what I believed needed to be done was all part of my conviction that we had to live differently – more lightly on this single planet of ours, more harmoniously and less wastefully. Without an overarching framework, each initiative's impact remains small. But if every government minister and every public service were striving to deliver a new world order, nothing would be impossible. We can all dream; what most people don't get the chance to do is to take their lives' passions – if that is not too grand a term – and turn them into national policies or laws.

Most of what I've described so far is related to my upbringing and experience and the choices I made therein as I grew into my beliefs – and it is absolutely true that we are all formed from that potent pot to a greater or lesser extent. However, looking back with the benefit of that old friend, hindsight, I can see clearly the two key moments that were to have the most profound influence in my life, both from 1992 – although I didn't discover either of them till later. The first was the Earth Summit and its ensuing Agenda 21 programme; the second was a book by Donella Meadows, *Beyond the Limits* co-written with Dennis Meadows and Jorgen Randers.

Epiphany #1: Agenda 21

The single most influential moment for me was discovering Agenda 21. This phrase articulated a commitment by 178 countries at the Earth Summit in Rio de Janeiro in 1992 to create a global action plan for sustainable development into the 21st century – hence 'Agenda 21'. Its first principle was, 'Human beings are at the centre of concerns for sustainable development. They are entitled to a healthy and productive life in harmony with nature.' This was a revelation to me. I was so excited when I first read this. Although it possibly ranks as one of the worst titles for a sustainability initiative ever, it was one of those epiphany moments when life suddenly made sense! For the first time I was seeing my two major passions, for social equality and the environment, come together. This is what I was going to do with my life.

Epiphany #2: Donella Meadows and systems thinking

Donella Meadows was key to my appreciation of the importance of systems thinking and the need to change the overarching system or framework of government in order to effect real policy revolution. In 1972 she and colleagues published *The Limits to Growth*, following a study initiated by the Club of Rome to look at the consequences of unchecked growth on a finite planet. The book sounded a major alarm and became the cornerstone of a global debate on how to achieve a sustainable future.

Written in the same year as Agenda 21, their second revolutionary book, *Beyond the Limits*, argued that society had gone into overshoot – a state of being beyond limits without knowing it: 'we are overshooting such crucial resources as food and water while overwhelming nature with pollutants like those causing global warming', and 'a sustainable future will require profound social and psychological readjustments in the developed and developing world'. I read this in 1998 and was confused. Of course, we knew this – that was what Rio was all about. But why hadn't governments acted on the information – or did they not want to know? I was heartened by her conclusion that there could be a peaceful restructuring of the 'system' to a sustainable society, but concerned that evidence and data were 'useful, necessary and not enough'. So what else was needed?

In her original book, *The Limits to Growth*, she had suggested that five softer tools, 'visioning, networking, truth-telling, learning and loving', could be really important. In her third book, *Limits to Growth, The 30-Year Update*, she said, 'these five tools are not optional; they are essential characteristics for any society that hopes to survive over the long term' and that 'each of these exists within a network of positive loops. Thus, their persistent and consistent application initially by a relatively small group of people would have the potential to produce enormous change – even to challenge the present system, perhaps helping to produce a revolution.'

I remember the hairs rising on the back of my neck when I read this. Could a marriage between evidence and empathy create a new political revolution towards creating more sustainable societies? What would be needed to achieve this? Could a law to protect future generations, for example, be a necessary component?

This also chimes strongly with the analysis of physicist Fritjof Capra, founder of the Center for Ecoliteracy at Berkeley. Fritjof reflects on the need to think systemically and identifies our failure to do so as a crisis of perception, which stops us acting as we should:

> *As the twenty-first century unfolds, it is becoming more and more evident that the major problems of our time – energy, the environment, climate change, food security, financial security – cannot be understood in isolation. They are systemic problems, which means that they are all interconnected and interdependent. Ultimately, these problems must be seen as just different facets of one single crisis, which is largely a crisis of perception. It derives from the fact that most people in our modern society, and especially our large social institutions, subscribe to the concepts of an outdated worldview, a perception of reality inadequate for dealing with our overpopulated, globally interconnected world.*

At the simplest level, my epiphanies were wake-up calls – a phrase I will use liberally to describe those moments of absolute clarity when you suddenly realise your own previous perceptions were wrong. To change perception, you have to change the system – and to change the system you have to change perception – essentially, systemic problems require new systemic solutions.

The making of the Well-being of Future Generations Act

It has now been five years since the Act came into law, and it is time to review it. I will draw on those who worked before me, with me and after me to bring the proposal from concept to legislation. I call on Welsh and international voices to comment on the Welsh journey and the opportunity for others.

I will link that journey to Donella Meadows' five key tools – from visioning (the ambition of the wild idea), to networking (the coalition of the willing that made it happen), truth-telling (daring to be honest about the challenge), learning (what is needed to be in place to make it happen) and loving (the embracing of the idea such that it encourages the best of us, rather than the worst).

The most important thing any law for future generations could do is to require that the legacy of each generation to its successors be the positive one of a just, resilient and ecologically sustainable society that will enable humanity not just to continue to exist but to flourish.

PROFESSOR KAREN MORROW,
Hillary Rodham Clinton School of Law, Swansea University

Through this book, and through varied international and intergenerational voices, I want to explore whether the concept of a legal 'golden thread' of intergenerational fairness, a law linking current and future generations, can reframe the system and tackle that crisis of perception. At its heart must be a debate around the role of government. In democratic constitutions, either unwritten as in the U.K., or written as in the US, the opportunity to legislate in the interests of 'posterity' or 'future generations' is there. After all, the very act of creating legislation is a long-term proposition, specifically designed to last longer than the current incumbency of government office.

My fundamental proposition is a simple one – that in a country that passes a law to protect the interests of future generations, the law in itself will drive different behaviours, both in *how* decisions are made and in *what* decisions are made. Such a law is a contract between a government and its people to actively look after their interests now and in the future. Surely all governments should want to do that? And surely, their populaces should seek such a commitment?

Other countries in the world are now taking notice. Here in the U.K., Lord John Bird's proposed U.K. Act, based on the Welsh Act, has started its parliamentary journey. There has also been interest in the Welsh Act so far from Canada, New Zealand, Portugal, Gibraltar, Australia and the United Arab Emirates. At stake for us all is the kind of future we want to bequeath the next generation – and the ones after that.

What happens next is up to you, the readers. If this frank account of the journey Wales has taken is useful in helping others learn, then this book will have been worth the effort; perhaps you will be encouraged to take more of your own steps towards living more sustainably. I hope at least some of you will demand similar legislation in your own countries – and if you do want to go down that route, there are many guiding voices in this book.

When I started this book with the proverbial empty page in front of me, I realised the truth of what many before me have said – life makes sense looking backwards. What at the time might seem inconsequential, you later realise was an essential part of making you who you are, of etching your core values on your soul. I can honestly say that my life, the experiences that have made me who I am, the people who have influenced what I believe, are all indivisible from the politician I became, and the person I am now.

Once you get the sustainability bug, you will find yourself on a lifetime of commitment to a roller-coaster ride against the tide, where for every step forward there will be more backwards. But just when you are feeling downhearted, some wonderful human being somewhere will give you hope – and off you go again.

'The making of successful legislation and policy often depends on timing as well as public and professional opinion. It is no coincidence that the Well-being of Future Generations (Wales) Act 2015 was supported not only in relation to environmental but also to social considerations.'

Catriona Williams OBE, CEO, Children in Wales

'Children are the guardians of our genome. Health and wealth of future generations relies on what priorities we give them today. A cultural shift in our society mediated through an integrated approach by governments, organisations, society and families is required whereby we prioritise 'our insurance policy' for better future by prioritising our children.'

Dr Layla Jader, MBChB, DA, MD (Wales), FMPHM, consultant in Public Health Genomics

'The old paradigm of "go to school, get a good job, and retire at age 65" is a relatively recent invention. I would argue that the protection of future generations lies in returning to the hero spirit of our ancestors. Ancestors who embraced the possibility of the unknown and who did so in community.'

Julie Wilson, Institute for the Future of Learning, US

CHAPTER 2

Visioning

The Journey to the Act, 1992–2011

*Visioning means taking off the constraints of feasibility, of
disbelief and past disappointments and letting your mind
dwell upon its most noble, uplifting, treasured dreams.*
DONELLA MEADOWS

The day we bought our home did not start well. Along with a small but stoical band, we were waiting in full wet-weather gear at a foggy Neyland Marina with rain lashing down and the wind rising for a decision as to whether the conditions would enable us to go dolphin hunting. This was not a regular sea-wildlife tourist tour, but a serious and regular attempt by a small and vigorous local charity, Seatrust, to record the numbers and varieties of dolphins in Cardigan Bay, which has some of the largest numbers of dolphins in the world. It was touch and go, but the captain of the *Cartlett Lady* was philosophical. The weather was meant to improve, and if we could negotiate Jack Sound successfully, we should be fine. Jack Sound is a treacherous, wild stretch of water with numerous reefs and a tidal race of 6 knots that has wrecked many an unwary ship. Jack made it hard for us that day, and we struggled our way through the old adage, 'Wind over tide makes for a rough ride.' But then we were clear, thrown vigorously out into the sea by Skomer Island (the bird reserve home of puffins and half the world's Manx shearwaters) and headed out to the Smalls – another famed shipwrecking site and into the Irish Sea – on our dolphin search.

We cruised gently for what seemed hours, binoculars at the ready for the telltale signs of gannets, the U.K.'s largest seabird, which feed by diving for fish at phenomenal speeds and which can often be seen feeding at sea in their hundreds. Today they were hidden in the swirling mist, but suddenly the sun broke through, the mist lifted and the water around us broiled and then exploded. What a sight: a pod of common dolphins, bowriding and leaping alongside us and under us. There were hundreds of them, playing cheekily, sleekly leaping, performing underwater somersaults with a sheer love of life – and loving the spectacle they were giving us. As quickly as they arrived, they left. I remember looking at the faces of our now very merry band lit up by the late-afternoon sun, glowing with the shared memory of something extraordinary – and my phone rang. It was the estate agent telling me that our offer on what is now our home had been accepted. This wild natural coast and sea was to become our new home, where we could live at one with nature, garden organically, forage and use nature as our energy source. Human beings having the right to live life in harmony with nature was advocated by the first Earth Summit in Rio in 1992. What we do not have the right to do as humans living now is to destroy nature and thus the potential for those who will live after us. Respecting the idea of humans living in harmony with nature is still the exception – it should be the norm.

How a duty became a promise

Wales is the first nation in the Western world to have a duty to promote sustainable development explicitly stated in its founding constitution, the Government of Wales Act 1998, thus rooted in the very law that created the National Assembly for Wales in 1999. This chapter explores how, within the lifetime of a generation, the early visioning of that duty subsequently came to be translated into the first legislation in the world to protect future generations.

I explore what such a radical (and progressive) approach means and how the context for decision making completely shifts when the needs and rights of future generations are taken into account. This is not about tick-box compliance in a traditional regulatory way, but a reframing of the idea of 'democracy for long-term good' by government and decision makers prepared to own the responsibility for decisions made now, by owning also their potential impact on the future – even if the full extent of the effects cannot be known.

Vision without action is merely day dreaming, action without vision is just passing the time of day; but combine action with vision and you can change the world.

NELSON MANDELA

The chapter also outlines the difficulty of delivering such a promise, despite a strong appetite for its delivery. Every such decision challenges the usual political orthodoxy and thus the traditional way of operating. Without the belt-and-braces approach of regulation, it is even more difficult. I explore the highs and the lows, the contribution from civil society (environmental bodies, campaigning organisations, charities) and the difficulty of maintaining a commitment to delivering on long-term aims under short-term political pressures. I also explore the importance of vision, values and narrative in weaving together a coalition of support, and hopefully demonstrate the opportunity of a small country to be more flexible in responding to such global challenges. I want this book to create lessons for others seeking to go down this path, and I hope that the frankness with which key actors have contributed will help that happen.

The context: U.K. sustainability policy, 1990–1999

It all started for me with the 1992 Earth Summit in Rio de Janeiro, which I described as my first epiphany in chapter 1. This was the first real attempt to catalyse a global sustainable development agenda, when world governments really appeared to be taking global challenges seriously; a time that felt extraordinary and full of promise for a new paradigm and new ways of working. The conference produced two key documents – the Rio Declaration on Environment and Development and Agenda 21, the global action plan for sustainable development into the 21st century. For the first time, global leaders accepted that the way governments usually operated in silos (responding to individual effects by identifying individual causes in individual sectors, rather than understanding the social, environmental and economic interdependences) was affecting the whole of the Earth's system. The key outcome was a set of organising principles for sustainable development to demonstrate their systemic interconnectedness. These principles created a framework for action to enable human beings to be at the centre of concerns for sustainable development, 'entitled to a healthy and productive life in harmony with nature'.

I think I can honestly say that Rio blew my mind! I had been suffering my own crisis of perception, not even understanding the interrelationship between the two key themes that were the most important to me – my passions for social equality and for the environment. I had seen the environment as my mainstay, being out in nature as my personal escapism, the gift that kept me grounded, rather than understanding that our not living in harmony with nature was at the core of our human problems. When I witnessed news stories about economic activities poisoning water, destroying forests and wildlife, I saw them as individual events to be resolved by governments, rather than as part of a wider extractive, economic model whose effects were then mostly unknown. And for the first time, the concept of inter-generational equity was placed at the heart of the Rio framework. This was huge! What was also significant was the specific recognition that identifying the interrelationship between society, economy and the environment was not enough; governments also needed to adopt procedural principles of transparency, information, participation and access to justice to test their success against the framework.

Following the Earth Summit at Rio, countries across the world agreed to make changes to the way they did business to reflect the Rio Declaration. The U.K. Conservative Government was first with its Sustainable Development Strategy in 1994. In 1997 the incoming

Visioning

U.K. Labour Government introduced a cross-government approach called Greening Government, linking environmental sustainability with economic and social progress. It established a new parliamentary scrutiny committee in the House of Commons – the Environmental Audit Committee (EAC). In 2000 it set up a new independent body, the Sustainable Development Commission, to work with all governments across the U.K. to monitor progress and build consensus on action to be taken by all sectors.

However, there was no clear idea in those early days of what 'good' looked like. It wasn't long before the Greening Government initiative was in trouble, criticised by both environment groups and explicitly by the new EAC for not providing 'sufficient leadership across government and the wider public service'. What is interesting with the benefit of hindsight – and hugely relevant to the Welsh story later – is that government effort went largely into the creation of new political structures without the consequent action or changes to policy delivery that external commentators, including the EAC, wanted to see.

In light of the external noise and challenge, the government tried again, with a bigger vision. In May 1999 the second Sustainable Development Strategy was published – 'A Better Quality of Life: A Strategy for Sustainable Development for the UK', with 'ensuring a better quality of life for everyone, now and for generations to come' as a strapline. It placed this 'at the heart' of decision making in the U.K. Government, adopting the Brundtland definition of sustainability (this is the most important term I will use in this book, and I talk about it below). Significantly, although it was called a U.K. strategy, in fact it was really an English strategy, recognising that the newly devolved administrations for Scotland, Wales and Northern Ireland would in due course develop their own objectives, priorities and indicators.

Devolution for Wales: 1997–1999

Following a referendum in 1997, devolution of powers from the U.K. Government to the new National Assembly of Wales, elected by the people of Wales, took place in 1999. At the time the new legislature was created, there was only a degree of self-government on offer. I say 'degree' because this first referendum offered only the very limited powers that had previously been held by the Secretary of State for Wales, who was part of the U.K. Government cabinet. The powers devolved to Wales were also substantially fewer than those devolved in the same year to Scotland or Northern Ireland, the other countries within the U.K. There was no opportunity in Wales to make new laws – that didn't come until much later – only to change regulations within a very small number of areas.

The devolution vote in Wales was won by the smallest of margins – less than 1 per cent. This was nail-biting stuff, particularly when you compare it with the large majorities in favour of devolution in Scotland (74 per cent) or for the Good Friday Agreement in Northern Ireland (71 per cent). The vote in Wales revealed a country split almost equally for and against greater self-determination – and that was those who voted at all. This close result occupied political commentators for years on the legitimacy of the National Assembly.

Introducing a duty to promote sustainable development

There had been no mention in the Government of Wales Bill (draft legislation) of a duty to promote sustainable development, but it was a live political issue in the context of the tussle between the EAC and the U.K. Government. In response, my councillor colleague Sue Essex (who was later to become the first cabinet minister with the responsibility for sustainable development in the National Assembly), working with the RSPB, proposed to the then–Secretary of State for Wales, Ron Davies, MP (Member of Parliament) – a keen bird-watcher – an amendment to place a duty on the new National Assembly for Wales to 'have regard' to the principle of sustainable development in all that it did. Reflecting back to that time, she told me, 'I was sick of hearing that there was an either/or approach to the economy and environment. There had to be a better way to consider not just environmental and economic objectives, but social welfare and justice objectives, which were frequently sidelined. The concept of sustainable development seemed to provide a prism through which these considerations could be thought through in a connected way.'

Sue is a great believer in collaboration and keen environmentalist. As the Government of Wales Bill was making its way through Parliament, she worked with others, notably the late Morgan Parry, then at the North Wales Wildlife Trust and the RSPB, to develop a prospectus for sustainable development which invited both individuals and organisations to sign up for the idea that a 'new Wales' could do things differently.

This was a very important rallying cry – and probably even more important were those who delivered it. It was civil society proposing the amendment, and it found a welcoming ear in the green, green grass of home in Wales. Interestingly, they were so successful in their lobbying that MPs decided the phrase 'due regard' was too woolly and proposed instead a strengthened approach of a 'duty to promote' in the final legislation. In doing so, Wales became one of only a very few governments in the world with any legislation to encourage sustainable development, despite the agreements that countries entered into at Rio. Without this far-sighted duty, and the work Sue and her colleagues did before the creation of the National Assembly, there would be no Well-being of Future Generations (Wales) Act now.

Section 121 of the Government of Wales Act 1998 states,

> *The National Assembly for Wales has* a duty to have a scheme *setting out how it will* promote sustainable development in the exercise of its functions *[emphasis added]*.

Not only was the new duty in itself worthy of note, but, following the approach outlined in Rio, the duty also contained a procedure to ensure that it would be delivered – a requirement to report on the implementation of the scheme and an assessment of how effective it had been. Combining a substantive policy commitment device with a procedural commitment device (if sufficient and robust) in this way can then drive the action needed to deliver on it.

This chapter will explore the journey through the first three Sustainable Development Schemes (as required by the Government of Wales Acts) towards the Well-being of Future Generations (Wales) Act. It will highlight the intrinsic pressures that are experienced by any government trying to change a paradigm, the importance of civil society in giving permission to government to think differently, and the creation of the conditions which ultimately led to my making the proposal for legislation.

The first scheme: 'Learning to Live Differently', 1999-2003

Nothing can quite prepare you for the moment you enter national politics. I've never had a prouder moment in my life than being elected by the people of Pontypridd as their first Assembly Member in May 1999. In the 1930s the very first woman MP in Wales, Megan Lloyd George (daughter of Prime Minister David Lloyd George), had been offered a chance to contest Pontypridd and famously said, 'Pontypridd is not ready for a woman.' I'm not sure it was when I became its candidate in 1998, either, as until the previous year Wales had only ever had four women MPs in the history of Parliament! But the new National Assembly was also a new beginning of a much more equal political representation, and I look back on my time in Pontypridd with love and affection.

One week after that first Welsh general election, I was delighted to be elected the first Deputy Presiding Officer (Deputy Speaker) of the new National Assembly and thus one of the two guardians of its rules of operation. That turned out to be absolutely the best job I could have had to learn the rules of engagement. A year later I was offered the cabinet responsibility for Education and Lifelong Learning, a portfolio I served in for seven years. As an ex-teacher passionate about learning and about education as a route out of poverty, I was over the moon! The theme of improving opportunities for current and future generations was right at the heart of my new role, and I was very keen to deliver my role in accordance with our unique sustainable development obligations.

Visioning

I had only been a minister for a matter of weeks before we were required to publish the National Assembly for Wales' first Sustainable Development Scheme, which we called 'Learning to Live Differently'. Led by Sue Essex, the scheme was co-drafted with the support of the Sustainable Development Commission chaired by Jonathon Porritt.

We adopted the most commonly used definition of 'sustainable development' from the Brundtland Commission, named for its chair, Gro Harlem Brundtland, and which was published in *Our Common Future* in 1987 by the World Commission on Environment and Development:

Development that meets the needs of the present without compromising the ability of future generations to meet their own needs.

Here the concept focuses on finding strategies to promote economic and social advancement in ways that avoid environmental degradation, overexploitation or pollution.

I've always liked this definition, as it describes an intention to really think about the consequences of the policy decisions you make, but it is not enough on its own to drive new kinds of behaviour and practice. There has to be a real commitment to action. We therefore further clarified it by saying: 'The Sustainable Development Scheme provides the overarching framework for all of the Assembly's work' and 'We will integrate the principles of sustainable development into our work and seek to influence others to do the same.'

A new vision for Wales

We wanted to become a new kind of government, celebrating and enhancing the fundamental characteristics of Wales – its environment, its strong sense of community, its bilingualism, its culture and heritage – but at our heart was the focus on tackling the key social equity issues that had led to Wales being the poorest nation within the United Kingdom. In particular, we wanted to be forward looking, to become a government with a new vision to excite and engage young people.

I loved this approach! It recognised the importance of creating the right environmental and social values to drive the culture of the new organisation and the need to lead by example. It was a visionary commitment ahead of its time, requiring a root-and-branch review of all decision making and policy actions. It was also a systemic approach that demanded we move away from traditional indicators and create new ones, bringing to the fore those that ameliorated the threats we were facing. As ministers, we wanted to create a new set of values at the heart of government *and* the public sector.

The commitment to becoming a place which 'values its children and where young people want to live, work and enjoy a high quality of life' was particularly important to me, as the way to get on in Wales has always been perceived as to get out. How many people across the world have been taught by Welsh teachers, cared for by Welsh nurses and doctors?

Setting sustainable development at the heart of government

In order to drive the agenda within the civil service, a Sustainable Development Unit was initially established in the Assembly's Environment Division to mirror the U.K. Government model. But locating both units in the environmental context confirmed what many believed – that sustainable development was solely an environmental issue. In the scheme launch debate, an amendment to change the arrangement was accepted, and the responsibility moved to the central Policy Unit, which sent out a clear signal about the intent to mainstream.

Two new bodies were established to assist in this mainstreaming: a Wales-based office for the new Sustainable Development Commission (SDC), and the Wales Sustainability Forum which later became Cynnal Cymru – Sustain Wales, a forum that was government-funded but independent, part of civil society. The creation of Cynnal Cymru provided an invaluable – and safe – place where serious matters focusing on ambition, action and accountability could be discussed in public and with politicians. Everyone was on a learning curve, so it was crucial to have direct engagement between politicians and civil society. World Wildlife Fund (WWF) was a key member, as were

Visioning

Wales Environment Link – the umbrella body for all the environmental charities in Wales – local government, public services and the social welfare non-government organizations (NGOs), who together were able to provide technical, strategic and delivery advice to the new government and act as critical friends.

Bringing in local government

Local government had previously embraced the Agenda 21 commitments and broadly welcomed this new focus, not least since it was their enthusiastic officers and members driving activity at the local level. There was an important two-way discourse between tiers of government and different sectors, for example local government officers advising civil servants and new ministers. This was vital on two levels – first that they had a breadth of experience that was not there in the civil service (because this was a new duty for them), and second that local government in particular was worried about the introduction of the new tier of government, the National Assembly for Wales. An agenda that played to their strengths on localism and expertise was important, and it also demonstrated a new collaborative approach which was very different from the way the civil service had previously worked. This was a core message about establishing a 'new Wales'.

Why was 'Learning to Live Differently' different?

At the core of the new approach was a set of commitments to govern sustainably, which meant:

- The environment being cherished and protected so that it remains healthy and biologically diverse, and can continue to support us all.
- A self-sustaining economy which respects the environmental and social context of Wales and responds to sustainable development opportunities.
- Action to make our communities strong and viable, and people healthier.

- People being enabled to play a part in taking decisions that affect them.
- Recognising the needs of all parts of Wales.
- Wales contributing to sustainable development at a global level as well as at a local.

This was a completely different agenda from any other part of the U.K. at the time, and it is interesting to note how close these core elements are to what have now become the goals in the Well-being of Future Generations (Wales) Act. Trying to achieve this approach has been a strong and continuing narrative for Wales since devolution.

Giving voice to our future generations

With my background in education, youth work practice and policy, I was particularly committed to establishing opportunities for young people to engage with the new National Assembly in the spirit of acting in the interest of future generations. In the first year I set about establishing a Children and Young People's Assembly for Wales through my role as Deputy Presiding Officer – later called Funky Dragon! This commitment, to enable young people to feed into the National Assembly and into government, has been an important theme in the development of the Wales' journey.

The idea of Wales as a policy and legal laboratory on children's rights and young people's empowerment – big enough to matter, small enough to be inventive – was first evidenced by the new National Assembly in Wales leading the way in the U.K. by signing the Convention on the Rights of the Child and the establishment of the first Children's Commissioner – policies that were soon followed by the other U.K. countries. These commitments were at the heart of my Education, Lifelong Learning and Skills portfolio, and the new context enabled me also to fulfil my dream of putting youth support services onto a statutory basis, not in a top-down way, but in discussion with young people. My support for these initiatives was directly linked to my fundamental belief in the voice of the next generation participating in and influencing policy development. For example, in 2004, a Welsh Youth Forum for Sustainable Development (WYFSD) was established following the second Earth Summit in Johannesburg. It was run by and for young people under 25 with an open membership and had a role not only in sharing representative expertise and experience with government but also in mobilising action amongst non-governmental audiences.

It was these commitments that at the time put Wales at the forefront of the UK and the European Union on youth policy – and ultimately on the pathway to the Well-being of Future Generations Act – with its commitment to young people and participation now enshrined in law. Now – as of a year ago – there is a formal Youth Parliament in Wales with elected representatives, mirroring the National Assembly itself, some of whose views are expressed on page 210.

First feedback

However, despite our efforts to establish the Assembly as a uniquely Welsh, responsible, forward-thinking legislature, it would be fair to say that it didn't need an effectiveness review to tell us that 'Learning to Live Differently' was not proceeding as planned. Our approach was described by Friends of the Earth in a press statement at the time as 'a commendable if utopian vision' but which read like an 'all things to all men wish list that is not easily grasped as a concept or a policy tool'.

There were probably a mix of reasons for such a big vision struggling to be heard. In hindsight I can see that many of the tools of delivery were not in place anyway. The shift taking place at that time within the Welsh civil service was a seismic one as it moved away from a body used to serving its London superiors; a body used to intermittent contact with the Secretary of State for Wales (who was usually not Welsh); a body which historically (since the Welsh Office had been set up in 1964) was mostly responsible for translating English policy into the Welsh context and language.

Now this small, democratically untested civil service was required to deal directly with newly elected and ambitious National Assembly

Members and a vibrant civil society – despite its previous lack of engagement with the body politic in Wales of local government, the public sector, business, the voluntary sector, communities and expert individuals.

It's also worth remembering that at the time we were all new politicians in a new, untried institution. As the only part of the U.K. with no primary powers – we couldn't make legislation at the time – and having been established by only a tiny majority, the risk of our being seen as a 'talking shop' was huge. We were perceived as politicians looking for a role; the Institute of Welsh Affairs, Wales' only independent think tank at the time, published a front cover to its magazine with all our pictures, describing us as 'the Great Unloved'.

The third key component was that old political dictum: 'Events, dear boy, events.' We may have had big ambitions about a new kind of legislature focused on being more sustainable, but in our first four years we faced a huge number of external crisis events – the loss of thousands of jobs from the steel industry, a tragic blast furnace explosion, major flooding, foot and mouth disease (which closed off access to the countryside for a year), a flu crisis and the Iraq War. Making more sustainable policies as a new core principle was severely tested in a crisis-response situation, in a new institution trying to get on its feet with very few powers at its disposal. One could argue this is a classic 'crisis of perception' response; however, had the sustainability agenda been fully embraced and in delivery, I would argue strongly that it would have helped us not only to make longer-term decisions from the beginning of the new institution, but also to better anticipate future problems, particularly those caused by unsustainable behaviour.

The second scheme: 'Starting to Live Differently', 2003–2007

If we'd been the 'Great Unloved' in 1999, we had become the 'Great Ignored' by 2003. The people of Wales were now well aware of how few powers we had and were either dissatisfied we didn't have more, or dissatisfied that we had any at all, particularly with the additional cost to the public purse of the extra democratic level. Voter turnout for the election was only 38 per cent, and less than half that was by people under the age of 35.

Reviewing the first scheme

As required by the Government of Wales Act, the incoming administration had to conduct an effectiveness review of the first Sustainable Development Scheme. The government commissioned its own review, the Davidoff Report. While those consulted welcomed and supported the overall approach, the study found that there was significant confusion in all sectors about the term 'sustainable development'. Several consultees found it hard to disassociate sustainable development from the more traditional 'green' agenda. This is a challenge that will appear time and time again.

As a result, many respondents to the Davidoff Report felt that key to delivering this challenging agenda in the Assembly's second term was to change people's attitudes and improve their understanding of both the meaning and the relevance of sustainable development. To facilitate this, participants in the study called for high-profile national information campaigns as well as further incorporation and embedding of sustainable development into the school curriculum. I was particularly delighted by this latter point . . .

What was abundantly clear was that respondents wanted ministers to provide a key leadership role in championing sustainable development, by leading by example, promoting best practice, influencing other organisations through our interactions with them, taking an international role and providing an overall vision for sustainable development in Wales.

Although the Davidoff Report was well respected, the fact that the government had commissioned it was a problem for civil society. The government agreed to conduct future effectiveness reviews externally. In the meantime Morgan Parry, now CEO of WWF in Wales and one of the initial promoters of the 'duty to promote', separately commissioned Dr Alan Netherwood, an academic with strong sustainability credentials, to review the scheme's effectiveness on behalf of civil society rather than the government.

Alan's review noted that the duty itself was popular among those who knew about it, particularly with NGOs, and there were warm tributes paid to Sue Essex AM as the political portfolio lead and Rhodri Morgan, the First Minister. However, while civil society organisations recognised the efforts being made, the most common evidence to the review demonstrated a lack of consistency of approach from both the civil service and ministers. Some had embraced it, while others explicitly had not. I well remember a conversation with a senior civil servant (not in my department) who told me when I questioned why his actions were a continuation of business as usual that once he was convinced that 'senior' ministers really required a different kind of delivery (ouch!), he would change his advice to his own department, but until then, he would not. I think that he was reflecting a common view, although most would not have been as frank!

Alan's report also noted a very significant point: that despite local authorities being obvious key allies with their experience and support for Agenda 21 and their advisory role to government, the Welsh Assembly Government had *not* required local government to demonstrate that they were mainstreaming sustainable development – nor indeed, any other public body. Critically, his report said that 'Learning to Live Differently' and its associated action plan did not provide an effective agenda for action for the Assembly and its partners.

Launching the second scheme with more leadership and more focus

'Starting to Live Differently' was the second Sustainable Development Scheme, launched in March 2004. On the front page was both a commitment – and a warning – by First Minister Rhodri Morgan to the civil service and public bodies in Wales: 'Sustainable development is not an option that will go away – it is the only way forward.'

With a new minister in charge, the second scheme aimed to make it absolutely clear that the National Assembly for Wales took this duty very seriously and ministers and civil servants were going to actively lead, as identified by the two effectiveness reviews. Carwyn Jones AM, the new Minister for Environment, Planning and Countryside, said: 'Sustainable development was still a new concept for government in those days and the accusation was that it was a fine aspiration in principle, but could not be followed in fact. This document aimed to start to change that thinking.'

Carwyn decided to focus this second scheme on specific actions to 'reflect the degree of leadership that our unique legal duty demands of us'. He acknowledged the difficulties in achieving the level of cross-disciplinary approaches required to deliver on the first scheme's big ambitions, not least due to the characteristic problems of Wales: a poor record on renewable energy generation (not unexpected for a country built on coal); a concern for the impact of reducing CO_2 emissions on its economy (its biggest industries being steel and air-craft manufacture); poor waste management, recycling and public transport provision and also greater historic economic inactivity, deprivation and inequality than most other European regions.

This second scheme contained 10 very specific commitments:

1. By 2010 all Assembly buildings will run on 100 per cent renew-able energy with an annual reporting structure, and we will work towards a similar figure for other public sector buildings.
2. All government agencies will report annually on the use of energy in their estates.
3. New public buildings must be built to the highest environmen-tal standards (Building Research Establishment Environmental Assessment Method [BREEAM] 'excellent' wherever possible).
4. The Assembly and its agencies will pilot renewables in Wales, including new solutions to tackle fuel poverty in homes.
5. The Assembly and its agencies will encourage indigenous microgeneration for businesses.
6. The Assembly will commission a project to promote the uptake of alternative fuels such as biofuels, biogas, natural gas and hydrogen.

7. EcoHomes energy-efficiency standards will be introduced. These standards are significantly above those required by building regulations for all new homes built by social landlords using the social housing grant.
8. A new agri-environment scheme will be introduced with wider environmental benefits across farm boundaries.
9. A Wales-wide, all-level strategy on education for sustainable development and global citizenship will be introduced.
10. New contract specifications for school meals must address health, nutrition and seasonality.

This revised, more focused scheme and action plan won praise from the Sustainable Development Commission for its emphasis on leadership and implementation as well as its participatory approach, engaging with local government and civil society as part of a wider agenda for system change. Jonathon Porritt, chair of the U.K.-wide Sustainable Development Commission, acclaimed 'the Assembly's unique clarity of vision and commitment to embed sustainability at the heart of everything by the end of the second term' but said in order to achieve that, the sustainable development principles *must* be embedded within both the Welsh Government and the public sector at the highest level, both horizontally across departments and vertically through public bodies and local government.

The new focus therefore was to deliver tangible outcomes across all our portfolios, with deadlines against which our performance could be measured. I was excited and keen to deliver my part, across all my responsibilities.

Beginning with education

I felt I had a particular obligation and opportunity as a Minister for Education, Lifelong Learning and Skills to contribute towards changing values and behaviour for the long term. I wanted to change the curriculum from the earliest school years right through to university level to reflect societal needs and challenges, including what science was telling us about climate change and the consequent need to live more sustainably. Since there is now a substantial evidence base demonstrating the importance of the early years in influencing the way we live our lives, I was determined to address this.

In Wales the vast majority of children go to state-run primary and secondary schools in their own communities. The school therefore has a hugely important role in the culture, identity and values of the cities, towns and villages of Wales and acts as a clear bellwether of the health, happiness and stability of our communities. The concept of community is also very strong, with many generations of families living in the same community.

In my regular visits to primary schools in Wales, it was quite clear that head teachers felt that the early years curriculum – up to seven years old – needed changing most urgently. The traditional desk-based teaching and regular testing introduced by the U.K. Government that children were experiencing from the age of five was not engaging many young children positively in education. We therefore proposed to create a new Foundation Phase curriculum (for three-to-seven-year-olds) for a new Wales, building on international research on curriculum and teaching methods to achieve an appropriate balance between the cognitive development of children and their emotional and social development through the creative potential of play and child-centred activities.

Outdoor learning played a key role – for example, the new curriculum introduced a new focus on children experiencing, through enquiry and investigation, the familiar world where they must 'learn to demonstrate care, responsibility, concern and respect for all living things and the environment'. I'm delighted to say that in 2011, the Foundation Phase's cross-disciplinary areas of learning approach (rather than the traditional, individual subject model of maths, English, geography, et cetera) became the formal national curriculum for early years in Wales; the rest of the curriculum up to school-leaving age will follow suit by 2022. I still chuckle at the memory of my favourite-ever press headline in response to my early outdoor learning endeavours:

'Minister makes children play in the rain'. We did – and proudly – and I hope future ministers will continue to do so.

What we also delivered was the uniquely Welsh commitment to make Education for Sustainable Development and Global Citizenship (ESDGC) a statutory part of the Welsh curriculum across all education sectors. This was my Education, Lifelong Learning and Skills contribution to deliver the specific commitment in 'Starting to Live Differently'. The Welsh Curriculum Authority worked with Oxfam and other development partners to write an imaginative global learning curriculum to ensure students at school, college and university understood their place in the world, and created resources for schools to enhance staff and students' understanding of sustainable development.

Beyond education: Wales, the world's first Fairtrade nation

This theme was further underpinned by another Wales innovation: our new 'Wales for Africa' initiative, which was particularly close to my heart – you may take the girl out of Africa, but you can't take Africa out of the girl. This started in 2005 as a targeted way in which Wales could contribute independently towards the UN-agreed Millennium Development Goals (MDGs), which aimed to dramatically reduce poverty in developing countries. We launched a campaign to make Wales the world's first Fairtrade nation (the Fairtrade Foundation's newest designation) to encourage ethical production in developing countries. The criteria were onerous: all our cities had to have active Fairtrade groups, along with 55 per cent of our towns and 60 per cent of our universities and schools. In addition, 75 per cent of people in Wales needed to know about Fairtrade products.

In June 2008 Wales did become the world's first Fairtrade nation. This was a very important message globally about what the new brand of Wales was becoming, and the culmination of a fantastic three-year campaign led by civil society organisations. It was also a real demonstration of people across Wales coming together in a common purpose. As the minister with the responsibility to help make it happen, I spent many months on the road, meeting amazing people and happily eating

Visioning

Fairtrade products for Wales! What I found on those visits the length and breadth of our nation was a real appetite for Wales to be more ethically responsible and environmentally sustainable.

Measuring change

On the civil service basis that if you can't measure it, it won't happen, I needed to ensure that the new global learning curriculum we were introducing, Education for Sustainable Development and Global Citizenship, was inspected in the same way as the rest of school activity. My experience in trying to do this became an important piece of learning that directly influenced the approach I took later in crafting the proposal that became the Well-being of Future Generations (Wales) Act.

We mandated our external independent inspection regime, Estyn, to require school inspection reports to comment on their ESDGC activity. This was not without some resistance by the inspectorate, who were at pains to point out that there was no common agenda or delivery and they did not have sufficient expertise. I understood the concerns but, making it clear that this was going to be at the heart of Wales' new education system, I dug in my heels and required Estyn to provide guidance to inspectors about how to assess the activity. We published *ESDGC: A Strategy for Action* providing the actions necessary for all education sectors, including universities, to enable the implementation of ESDGC.

Believing in change

I also realised that although huge efforts were being made by *some* civil servants and *some* ministers, this was not yet enough to change old behaviours. To make change effective, you need to change the culture of operation. If mainstreaming is representing 'the prevailing current of thought, influence, or activity' or 'the prevalent attitudes, values, and practices of a society or group' (both definitions from the Free Dictionary), then clearly in Wales at that time, the debate had not been won. Despite our efforts, our government focus was still perceived to be on process not delivery – in other words, the structures rather than the outcome. Yes, there was substantial activity, and some practices had changed, but not the attitudes and values of the National Assembly for Wales itself. No wonder that by the end of the Assembly's second term, the Welsh Sustainable Development Commissioner, Peter Davies, commented that 'the rhetoric is outweighing the tangible process by some degree' despite 'a myriad of speeches, reports, action plans and strategies'.

A second Government of Wales Act in 2006 gave Wales enhanced legislative powers after the next election – from the beginning of the next government. For those readers who lap up constitutional changes, the critical change was to alter the status of the National Assembly for Wales from being a corporate body (with no separation between the government and the legislature) to the usual structure: a government (albeit one with limited legislative powers) and a separate legislature. This meant that from 2007 the sustainable development duty fell solely to the incoming government, not to the members of the National Assembly. In short, the Welsh Government is bound by the duty now; the National Assembly is not.

The third scheme: 'One Wales, One Planet', 2007–2011

The third Assembly election took place in May 2007. It is extraordinary to reflect back on this, but until that moment, like most other administrations, we had no minister with a responsibility for climate change. Prior to the election campaign, I had been lobbying Rhodri Morgan hard to address this, calling for a minister to have responsibility for sustainable development, climate change, biodiversity, planning, buildings, water, environment, waste, recycling, energy, infrastructure – a brief where you could make a real difference on the ground at the Welsh national level. When I was invited to join the next cabinet, I was offered the brief I'd proposed – Environment, Sustainability and Housing, including all responsibilities related to the title and in addition, responsibilities for national parks, footpaths, recycling, litter and my secret favourite – the development of eco-schools. This actually came as a huge surprise to me, as I was lobbying for the role to be created, but not for myself! However, such a large interconnected brief was a huge opportunity to take coherent action to deliver on our sustainability commitments across a wide range of government responsibilities. My portfolio was equivalent to seven U.K. Government ministers, but with only about 5 per cent of their staff to support me, which is both the challenge and the opportunity of a small country. I was determined to do as much as possible in line with our sustainability commitments.

We were now in coalition with Plaid Cymru, and political arithmetic meant that together we formed a large majority. The opportunity to deliver change was therefore hugely enhanced. We agreed on a coalition manifesto for action, 'One Wales', made up of some of our election commitments and some of theirs. I was delighted that there was common ground between the two parties in recognising that 'climate change is the greatest threat facing humanity' and committed Wales, with its high carbon legacy, to be at the forefront of reducing carbon by 3 per cent a year from 2011. This was the basis for my establishing an all-party and expert reference group to create the plan to deliver – the Welsh Climate Change Commission.

A people's vote for a Welsh law

Prior to the 2007 election, additional powers had been granted to the National Assembly in the second Government of Wales Act – still not primary legislative powers, but including a rather colonial mechanism whereby ministers could ask for primary powers in specific circumstances agreed by the U.K. Government. However, this was a major move forward in responsibilities for the Assembly, so the Welsh BBC tried to galvanise interest in the third Assembly elections by running a people's competition for a new law, which a member of the public would propose and which all parties promised they would 'consider' if they became ministers.

In a small country, a public opportunity like this tells you quickly what level of support you will have for an initiative. After the public vote, it was down to two propositions: banning smacking and banning plastic bags – somewhat ironically, both were beyond the new legislative powers granted to Wales at that time. Although both proposals had their detractors, they symbolised a public appetite in favour of changing laws to encourage more environmentally and socially sustainable behaviour. I was supportive of both but was selfishly delighted that the winner was the banning of plastic bags. What a gift to a minister in a new portfolio who hates waste as much as I do! This was a huge fillip to persuade the civil service and the Welsh public that the new Assembly would tackle issues of importance to the public. The U.K. Government was clear that we would not be given the powers to ban plastic bags, but, buoyed up by the support for the proposal, I was able to take decisive action in the spirit of the public vote; Wales was therefore the first country in the U.K. to introduce a 5p charge on each plastic bag, which brought their use down by 90 per cent in the first year and created a large income for environmental charities. Within four years the rest of the U.K. followed Wales' lead. I'm pleased to say that as I write, Welsh Government legislation has also gone through the National Assembly to remove the defence of 'reasonable chastisement', in other words to ban smacking – another key policy in the interests of future generations.

Epiphany #3: we have only one planet

My personal journey to the creation of the Well-being of Future Generations Act really started with an epiphany moment that took place in October 2007. I was invited by Morgan Parry, CEO of WWF Cymru, to speak at the launch of WWF's report 'One Planet Wales'. This report and the event changed my life politically and personally. Using the concept of the ecological footprint (how much biologically productive land and water an individual, population or activity requires to produce all the resources it consumes and absorb the waste it generates, measured in global hectares), the report calculated that if everyone in the world consumed natural resources and generated carbon dioxide at the rate we do in Wales, we would need at least three planets to support us.

Visioning

The report concluded that we must cut Wales' ecological footprint by 75 per cent by 2050 in order to live within our fair share of the planet's resources. Importantly, it also showed the way to deliver a 'One Planet Wales' through reducing the footprint of eight key sectors – food, buildings, transport, products, services, energy, resources and our lifestyles – with recommendations for the short, medium to longer term from 2007 until 2050.

Until this point I had not realised just how much of an impact our personal choices made on our futures. I made the decision there and then, actively supported by my family, to calculate our family footprint and actively reduce it as much as possible. So from a start of changing to a renewable energy company (energy); our house is now fully insulated (buildings); we walk, cycle, use public transport and drive electrically (transport); we buy items only when we need them – and second-hand if possible (products); we grow as much of our own fruit and vegetables as we can (food); increasing biodiversity on the way (resources); we try to avoid air miles on products delivered and support local providers (services) and the quality of our lives has substantially improved (lifestyles) as we are becoming part of the solution, rather than part of the problem.

As a government, we had already been using the ecological footprint as a high-level indicator since the introduction of 'Starting to Live Differently' in 2004, but I was still struggling to explain what a more sustainable Wales could look like on the doorstep and why it was important. Somehow we needed to enable more people to understand the impact of their choices so they too could actively decide to live more lightly on the planet. This gave me the beginning of an idea. What I particularly liked at the time was the ease with which you could use the ecological footprint as a shorthand way to describe our current problem to anyone, given we clearly only have one planet available to us: a concept that three-year-olds have no difficulty in understanding, even if some world leaders don't!

As a minister, I needed to take the same approach to footprint reduction in my portfolio, hopefully with other ministers in support. One of the most frightening findings of the 'One Planet Wales' report was that if current trends and existing policies were followed, Wales' footprint was projected to increase by 30 per cent, mainly due to growth in air travel and the food and drink sector, when we needed to reduce it by 75 per cent. This was clearly going in the wrong direction, and particularly for a country with a sustainable development duty! We commissioned the Stockholm Environment Institute at the University of York, specialists in footprint analysis, to look at scenarios to 2020 to inform our next policy steps.

The review of the second scheme

The key recommendation of the Effectiveness Review in 2008 was to instruct the government in its third scheme to 'create a route map for sustainable development which sets out what a sustainable Wales would look like with clear emphasis on how we will get there'. Building-ing on the big-vision approach in 'Learning to Live Differently' and the more targeted approach in 'Starting to Live Differently', this was music to my ears. It explicitly gave me, as the responsible minister, the opportunity to articulate both a vision and a delivery plan for what a more sustainable Wales would look like. The concept of 'One Wales, One Planet' was born. The coalition partnership between the two political parties, Labour and Plaid Cymru, meant it was really important that it was not *my* vision or *my* plan, but a vision agreed by both parties and as many stakeholders as possible in the new Wales way. I used the Welsh Climate Change Commission as a vehicle to test ideas for a vision of a future Wales.

'One Wales, One Planet': the third scheme that inspired the Act

What I wanted to propose was a radical change – to be absolutely explicit about what sustainable development meant in practice in both policy development and delivery across the whole of government. I had two guiding factors: I wanted our approach to be very different from a traditional government document, so I wanted inputs from civil society, environmental and climate experts from NGOs and universities, businesses and young people. I also wanted it to inspire people of all ages by laying out a vision of a better, kinder, more tolerant future; a future where there was a paradigm shift away from the unicorn of infinite growth, away from our headlong dash for carbon, and towards the importance of community, of kindness, of a more responsible relationship with nature – a focus on what really matters. I wanted to propose a new strategic framework to be *the* overarching strategic aim of *all* Welsh Government policies and programmes, across *all* ministerial portfolios, making sustainable development the central organising principle of government, rather than a key theme which then had to compete with others.

Epiphany #4: incrementalism doesn't work

I spent hours promoting the ideas across Wales and internationally in formal and informal meetings. One of my biggest influencers and advocates was Andy Middleton, an entrepreneur who is passionate about living more sustainably. Andy's strapline then and now is that we are not moving at the scale and pace commensurate with the challenges we face. On one occasion, as deputy chair of Cynnal Cymru, he was chairing an event I was opening as minister. Earlier that day I had negotiated additional money to help more children learn to cycle in school, and I proudly announced that children in 20 per cent of Welsh communities would now benefit from school cycling lessons. Andy responded as chair by asking me, 'So how many children do you not want to see cycling, Minister? What about the other 80 per cent?' I realised that he was absolutely right. I was working in a political environment where ministers would make small beneficial announcements and get good local news stories. Andy on the other hand was rightly challenging me as to why I believed that if it was good enough for 20 per cent of schoolchildren, shouldn't it be made available to all? This was an important challenge, as it immediately changed my level of ambition – and changing your ambition can completely change your focus.

#futuregen

Winning the argument

I was determined to persuade all those who had put time and effort into supporting the previous schemes that we were serious about lifting our commitment to the next level; that we understood why the previous schemes had failed – and it was mostly about competing priorities. We had learned from the effectiveness reviews and now we were coming back to them with a clear sense of direction and a very specific commitment to make sustainability *the central organising principle* of government. We were going to be clear, we were going to be radical and we were going to deliver.

First, I had to convince the First Minister, Rhodri Morgan. He had no problem with radical proposals – but he insisted on them being well argued. Rhodri had always been a very strong supporter of the sustainability agenda and, like me, he was concerned that government delivery in practice was not living up to our ambition. He felt that the time was right to be more interventionist and to send a very clear message to politicians, the civil service and wider partners.

Once I'd secured his backing, I talked to all the ministers individually to gain their support and – still with some trepidation – took my proposal to the cabinet. There I was delighted to secure unanimous support! 'One Wales, One Planet' proposed that using the ecological footprint, 'within the lifetime of a generation, we wanted to see Wales using only its fair share of the Earth's resources', and we would use all our means to address this. If this approach was also supported by the public services and by civil society, it had the potential to be transformative. Also significant was that it created a vision of a country that was care-full for its people and of its environment, actively enhancing the opportunity for 'human beings to have the right to live in harmony with nature', as outlined in the Rio Declaration.

I still think that 'One Wales, One Planet' is one of the most important, most radical and most well-argued documents I've ever read from a government – and worthy of others on their own journeys taking a look. It is not my document – I had the most excellent team of committed civil servants to thank for its drafting along with a real collective impetus from Morgan Parry, Peter Davies, Cynnal Cymru, the Welsh Climate Change Commission and wider civil society, but I was proud to put my name to it. It lays out a vision, which I give in full in appendix 1, for a more sustainable Wales as a country that:

- Lives within its environmental limits.
- Has healthy, biologically diverse and productive ecosystems that are managed sustainably.
- Has a resilient and sustainable economy.
- Has communities which are safe, sustainable and attractive places for people to live and work, where people have access to services, and enjoy good health.
- Is a fair, just and bilingual nation, in which citizens of all ages and backgrounds are empowered to determine their own lives, shape their communities and achieve their potential.

To achieve this, sustainable development will be *the central organising principle of the Welsh Government, and we will encourage and enable others to embrace sustainable development as their central organising principle.*

Uniquely Welsh

It's important to say that through 'One Wales, One Planet', for the first time, we were applying sustainable development principles widely, across all our activity, but in a uniquely Welsh way. I support the argument that sustainable development should have a common understanding the world over, which is why we used the Brundtland definition, but in becoming a guiding principle for an individual country, it has to be located in the spirit of that country's culture and place. It was critical therefore that Wales' approach to sustainable development should be based on the contribution of its land and people, and rooted in our rich and diverse culture, supporting and sustaining our traditions, languages and heritage. This was an agenda close to my heart and very strongly supported by civil society.

'One Wales, One Planet' for the first time used 'the well-being of Wales' as a key indicator for sustainable development, with evidence drawn from the fairness of our society, lifelong learning, language and culture. The core principles that underlined the agreed vision were those that were subsequently translated legally into the provisions of the Well-being of Future Generations (Wales) Act, which also explicitly included 'culture' as one of the four underpinning domains alongside environment, society and economy. I am firmly of the belief that having this broader understanding is critically important in bringing other countries to the table in a way that explicitly recognises their own cultures and traditions.

Launching 'One Wales, One Planet'

In May 2009 First Minister Rhodri Morgan launched 'One Wales, One Planet' at the Hay Festival, the internationally renowned literature festival. He said: 'Our Scheme for Sustainable Development gives Wales the opportunity to show leadership and ambition, and to learn from the past. It gives us the opportunity to show how we are playing our full role as a global citizen within the context of the UN MDGs.'

We deliberately chose the Hay Festival to launch the scheme, as the festival brings together global writers, leaders and thinkers for challenging, stimulating and inspiring conversations. It was not a usual government setting and was (and still is) a festival exemplar in reducing its footprint. Every year the Hay Festival welcomes a profusion of global specialist climate and nature-related speakers, yet there was an almost complete absence of anyone from the worlds of government and business with work hats on to learn from experts and one another. A conversation between Andy Middleton and Andy Fryers, the sustainability director at the Hay Festival, led to the start of a new series of sustainability-related events at the festival: 'Hay on Earth', now #GreenHay. The first two years of events brought government ministers, local authority chief executives, business leaders, environmental NGO directors and concerned citizens to learn, plan and commit to action. The creation of a 'safe space' for the Welsh Government to witness, share and test policy ideas led to a series of Green Dragons' Den events where community enterprises, charities and start-ups could pitch sustainability ideas to a panel of Welsh Government and other specialists for a government-funded financial reward to take ideas forward. This was exciting, inclusive, innovatory and is why this book is also being launched (virtually, due to Covid-19) at the Hay Festival, five years after the Well-being of Future Generations (Wales) Act has become law.

A core change to enable delivery?

With civil society keen to engage on delivering the vision outlined in 'One Wales, One Planet', and with public sector partners such as the health, education and environment services broadly supportive of the change, we still had to ensure delivery from the government itself. Each effectiveness review had made clear that there was not an effective delivery mechanism across the civil service, so we created a new key civil service role, Director General for Sustainable Futures, and a new policy integration tool to engage across government.

We established an internal network of sustainable development advocates with representatives from all ministerial departments, who acted as champions to raise the profile in their respective areas. We also made it absolutely clear that 'living within environmental limits' was recognised as the prerequisite to ensure that economic and social progress can be maintained into the future. This is a core theme of 'One Wales, One Planet': that environmental limits provide a real constraint, a threshold on what is sustainable or not.

In order to take a belt-and-braces approach, the new Director General, Clive Bates, and I went to see each minister individually to discuss with them what their understanding of their role was and what our expectations were of them. This took some time but was a really valuable exercise in promoting the agenda as good government and governance. It was particularly important to me to have buy-in from ministers with public sector, economic and financial responsibilities.

We took a short paper that Clive had written, and agreed with my views, to tackle the issue of what sustainable development meant – and how to make it useful, which I recap here:

Sustainable development is a widely used and often abused term. However, it is both possible and desirable to use the concept of sustainable development in Wales, but only if three conditions are met:

1. There must be clarity in the meaning of sustainable development.

To qualify as a 'central organising principle' for a government or country, the concept must be very widely applicable and make sense when applied as an agenda that spans health, the economy, education, environment, planning et cetera.

*Drawing on the definitions used in 'One Wales, One Planet', we propose that the outcome from sustainable development should be **maximisation of well-being over the long term** as an overall goal – a 'super-outcome' to which all other outcome objectives contribute.*

*It is not primarily a 'green' idea – **it is a broad concept** that covers all the components of well-being: health, employment, community and social relations, et cetera.*

***It stresses long-termism** – focusing on the full life course and the well-being of people in the future – it makes us think of natural, human, social, economic capital as an endowment.*

*We care about **the distribution of well-being and fairness**, placing greater emphasis on people with poor well-being and tackling misery.*

*There is a good and growing **evidence base** about well-being drivers.*

2. It must inform hard choices in policy and investment.

We argue that pursuit of well-being does surface hard trade-offs: for example in allocation of resources to long-term well-being at the expense of shorter-term investments. It can mean breaking down

silos, better integration and service redesign. It requires a determined evidence-based approach and focus on cost-effectiveness.
Generally, we might expect this to mean:

> Greater focus on **prevention / early intervention**: with
> manifestations in health, criminal justice, environment and
> energy, family policy, education et cetera.
>
> More attention to **dealing effectively with failure**, as this
> has long-terms costs and consequences. For example, do we
> focus enough on kids who are going wrong at school?
>
> **More integration across silos** – for example, so that we have
> the right links between National Health Services (NHS)
> and social care to avoid bed-blocking, better handling
> of transition (for example, when someone comes out
> of prison), use of farming practices rather than water
> treatment for water quality.
>
> **Greater focus on mental health** and recognition of drivers of
> well-being in, say, planning where greater weight could be
> given to securing housing supply.

3. It must be possible to secure sufficient public acceptance.

A government practising sustainable development will need to
be aware of the 'elastic limit' of the bond between government and
citizens – and this places a constraint on how far and fast it is
possible to introduce change – for example, in cutting emissions,
charging polluters, redistributing wealth et cetera. A government
seeking to secure buy-in to sustainable development would:

> Seek to make larger changes over a longer period – **'slow, big
> wins'**. Governments overestimate what they can achieve in
> the short term and underestimate what they can achieve in
> the long term.
>
> **Promote behaviour change** – use techniques from
> behavioural science and economics to change attitudes,
> motivation and behaviour.

> **Build trust** – *for example, through external scrutiny, indepen-*
> *dent advice, openness.*
> **Create compelling narratives** – *explain what we are doing*
> *and how we change Wales for the better.*

I thought – naively – we had now cracked the problem: we had a senior civil service lead and the policy approach was clear, led by the First Minister and agreed on by all the cabinet. We would be delivering it in partnership with the whole public sector. Local government had told us they were fully on board. We had created the conditions, the collegiality, to encourage this dialogue, challenge and experimentation; we were world-leading in our ambition. I could get on with my part of delivery and anticipate that others would do theirs. Together we would build a more sustainable Wales.

Awakenings

I spent the next year trying to ensure that I was active in every aspect of my portfolio. We were able to demonstrate in our own annual review that we had met or embedded all our previous scheme commitments. For the first time it felt that the agenda was being taken seriously – that the message had been taken throughout the organisation; that every portfolio in the Assembly government was doing something. Rhodri as First Minister had made it clear to cabinet colleagues that I was carrying out my functions on his behalf, rather than as a portfolio minister. And yet somehow, it just didn't feel to me very different from business as usual. I witnessed a huge amount of effort going in and a substantially increased use of the rhetoric, but the fundamental direction of travel did not seem to me to be changing.

Wake-up call #1

The Wales Audit Office published a damning report, *Sustainable Development and Business Decision Making in the Welsh Assembly Government*. It commended a number of initiatives, including those I'd been closely involved in, such as the 'Wales for Africa' programme, the ESDGC curriculum and our healthy school meals approach, and recorded that the Welsh Assembly Government had complied with its statutory commitments (in the promotion of sustainable development). But in terms of embedding sustainable development as the central organising principle, it found that for the civil service, the agenda was seen as 'one of a number of competing priorities' rather than 'the means by which the Assembly Government managed its competing priorities'.

The report highlighted problems with the culture of the organisation which inhibited integration, had not challenged 'business as usual', had not tackled silo working and had no performance accountability. In particular, the report highlighted that the Welsh Assembly Government had created indicators that reported on the progress of Wales but not of its own performance.

Although the majority of the fieldwork of the audit office had taken place prior to the launch of 'One Wales, One Planet', this was a huge wake-up call, the first of three that led to my proposing legislation to embed the central organising principle in law.

In many ways for me, the worst aspect of it was to find out that despite my many meetings with the top of the office – the most senior civil servants – government staff lower down in the organisation had never been told about the commitment to sustainable development as the central organising principle and were not being required to change their behaviour. Effectively, the frenetic activity which I and the colleagues who really supported this approach had taken was in our own silo – exactly the issue we were hoping to address through mainstreaming.

The internal network of civil service sustainable development advocates charged with the mainstreaming role was populated by very committed people, but it became clear that for the most part, these advocates did not have the leverage or resources internally to mainstream sustainable development across their departments. System change was not happening.

There was a similar story in local government. As a result of 'One Wales, One Planet', an external network was set up – the Sustainable

Development Coordinators Cymru. This exhibited the same problem as our internal network – all excellent people, but relatively junior. Most came from environmental backgrounds rather than being located centrally in the chief executive's office, which once again pigeonholed sustainability as an environmental agenda.

This was a key point in my understanding of the way governments work. I now realised that a cabinet-agreed commitment was not enough in itself. It was necessary, but not sufficient. Knowing I had the full backing of the soon-to-be-retiring First Minister Rhodri Morgan, I felt conned. I remember cycling home uphill on a rotten night where the skies mercilessly contrived to soak me to the bone and getting home absolutely wet through to find there was no hot water – pathetic fallacy in action! I couldn't sleep that night. What would it take to make the approach work? The new First Minister Carwyn Jones was as supportive as Rhodri Morgan had been but similarly relied on me to set the ministerial direction and sort it out.

Embedding the principle

The relationship between ministers and civil servants in the U.K. has fairly strict parameters. Ministers set direction; the civil service delivers ministerial priorities and legal obligations. This is key – although I didn't realise how key at the time. As there had been no explicit manifesto commitment, or explicit coalition commitment through the 'One Wales' coalition document to make sustainable development *the* central organising principle – the civil service still did not see the commitment as *the* priority among other priorities even though the cabinet had endorsed it. From the civil service perspective, the Wales Audit Office had made it clear that, although the commitment was not embedded as agreed in 'One Wales One Planet', the Welsh Assembly Government had in fact complied with its legal commitments under the Government of Wales Acts to promote sustainable development in the exercise of its functions. I had more work to do.

The Sustainable Development Commission representative for Wales, Peter Davies, helpfully wrote to me to recommend that, because the Wales Audit Office is the lead auditor of government, sustainable development was now going to have to be its central organising principle as well. This is a really important point for those looking to embed sustainable development as the central organising principle; it is not just about changing the culture of the government – politicians and civil servants – it is also about ensuring that all the monitoring and evaluation mechanisms and accountability indicators are also changed to become the foundation of the new approach to government planning, policy development and spending decisions.

I decided on a twin-track approach: for there to be a specific civil service training programme delivered via the Director General for Sustainable Futures, and for me to actively create a coalition of the willing to communicate the vision for a more sustainable Wales across Wales in partnership with Cynnal Cymru. This approach centred on capitalising on the tremendous support I had from organisations outside government and actively bringing them in to work with us.

One of the new initiatives that arose out of this was the Sustainable Development Charter, the purpose of which was to encourage new behaviours in businesses, charities and civil society. I was particularly excited about the opportunity of the charter as a public commitment that external organisations could make by signing up to making sustainable development their central organising principle and committing to reporting annually on how they were faring. I think a mechanism such as this is a critically important one, particularly if it is made a condition for receipt of government funding. There was a lot of good feedback on this approach, the most positive benefit of which was the sharing of good practice and learning across sectors – private, voluntary and public sectors.

Wake-up call #2
The second wake-up call followed hot on the heels of the first. A year after 'One Wales, One Planet' was launched, WWF went back to Alan Netherwood to report on the 'Progress of Embedding the "One Planet" Aspiration in Welsh Government'. Using the Welsh Government's own

commitments, Alan's report looked at whether the government policy agenda was fit for the purpose of delivering the ambitious structural change needed.

Despite our public commitment, the report noted disappointingly, 'One Wales, One Planet' was *not* featuring in the policy discourse, particularly in economic development, the public sector, transport and housing, although it was featuring strongly in food and agriculture, energy, and waste. Was this because the two of us in the latter portfolios were more committed? Or was it because big portfolios will always contain a crisis, so you need to be very determined to keep a new narrative against the odds? It would be fair to say that ministers with economic portfolios often found it the most difficult to engage because the pressure of maintaining business as usual is immense. The report asked and answered a really important question: 'Is all the admirable effort reviewed in this report stemming footprint growth or even beginning to reduce it. The short answer is we just don't know.' As the Wales Audit Office had done, Alan Netherwood suggested a need for greater accountability, scrutiny, monitoring of performance as well as a route map for long-term, high-level strategy.

I was really disappointed by these two critically important reports. I thought that all the work that had gone into 'One Wales, One Planet' from such a large number of people would have made a difference. Yet instead of sustainable development being *the* central organising principle as we'd agreed, not only was it still one of many competing priorities, but it was not even generally part of our public discourse and engagement! Essentially, I had failed, despite a unanimous political commitment by the cabinet. What these two reports did was to harden my resolve, but I needed to reconsider my approach. How could we require the government to deliver better politically and organisationally?

Regulation, regulation, regulation!

When Alan Netherwood reported, we had just introduced a new regulatory approach to tackle waste by vastly increasing and standardising municipal recycling. I was spending a lot of my time meeting with local authorities (who had the responsibility for household recycling and waste services) proposing the new agenda and, important in this context, new regulatory targets with fines for non-compliance. The meetings were not easy, as local authorities take their autonomy on service delivery very seriously. However, this was a really important dialogue about jointly creating a 'slow, big win' which would demonstrate the value of the central organising principle approach. It took months of discussions, evidence based academic papers and financial discourse before we agreed on the way forward. Through my regular engagement, evidence sharing, additional budget provision and the promise of sector-leading work, we eventually got there and mapped out a regulated future where local authorities were specifically required through waste prevention statutory targets to increase recycled materials and reduce landfill by specified amounts leading to 70 per cent reduction by 2025 and zero-waste by 2050.

In many ways this is the most important Welsh example of a major sectoral change consistent with the embedding principle. 'Towards Zero Waste' was a mission-driven agenda innovating through both regulation (which became progressively tougher over time) and a collaborative approach to what improvements should look like. It is also a useful success story, as, through this regulatory mechanism, Wales went from being one of the worst recyclers in the world to one of the very best in the world in a decade. The regulatory mechanism was the driver, as local authorities could then prioritise their own human and financial resources to delivering the agreed required outcomes.

We took a similar approach on introducing the first charge in any U.K. nation on single-use carrier bags. I had warned the supermarket retail sector that if the voluntary agreement they had entered into with the U.K. Government did not lead to a sufficient reduction, I would legislate to introduce a charge. They did not achieve the reduction, so I did legislate. Interestingly, although I had convened meetings annually with the supermarkets for three years up to my proposing legislation, the sector was not generally minded to send a representative to Wales to meet a regional government, and the fact I could, and would, legislate appeared to take the sector giants by surprise. Being able to demonstrate that they had been fully informed over a sufficient period of time was critical to avoiding court action to try to prevent our approach.

Wake-up call #3: the final trigger

The third wake-up call was the loss of the Sustainable Development Commission, ironically announced immediately following its 10th anniversary conference. There had been a general election in May 2010, following which a coalition between the Conservative Party and the Liberal Democrat Party formed a new U.K. Government and dispensed with the SDC without any discussion with the commission, the devolved administrations or indeed anyone else. As one of the conference speakers, I was incensed. This had to be the ultimate irony: the very body charged with the responsibility to advise all governments in the U.K. on better and longer-term decision making to look after future generations, dispensed with overnight with no consultation! I did not want to lose the expertise, so immediately established Peter Davies, the Wales-based commissioner, as a new Sustainable Futures Commissioner in Wales to act as an advocate for sustainable development and as a critical friend to Welsh Government – a role in which he excelled.

Towards legislation

This was the final catalyst that led me towards legislation. I was determined to ensure that all the efforts we'd made so far in Wales would bear fruit and that we would deliver both on our unique legal duty and the political commitment to embedding sustainable development as the central organising principle. If it was going to become the priority for the civil service, it had to be in the governing party's manifesto and to become a law. Since at no time did any external review say that we were not delivering on our obligations as required by the successive Government of Wales Acts, clearly that duty – the duty to promote

– was not enough. However, in the areas where I'd legislated, in relation to recycling and carrier bags, for example, the route, the benefits and the sanctions were clear. We needed to take a similar approach.

Over a 45-minute journey from England to Wales, I wrote what I believed would be the necessary architecture to underpin a regulatory approach to embedding sustainable development as the central organising principle, recognising the concerns raised in effectiveness reviews. We needed to turn the law from a duty to 'promote' to a duty to 'deliver'. We needed to define sustainable development so people understood what it was they were to deliver. Since the effectiveness reviews had all drawn attention to the lack of a government-wide mechanism, the government itself needed to be subject to such a law – so that the law could become the mechanism.

We needed external input from a commissioner with substantial powers, just as we'd previously created a Children's Commissioner, and the Wales Audit Office – as the primary auditor of public services in Wales – who would need to audit in a different way as a result of the law. In short:

- There should be an act requiring the Welsh Government and all its public sector organisations to make sustainable development their central organising principle.
- The Welsh Government itself should be subject to the Act.
- Delivery of the Act in the Welsh Government and public sector should be audited by the Wales Audit Office, which would need to make the Act's delivery its central organising principle.
- There should be a commissioner with substantial powers who would act as a critical friend and be able to hold organisations to account.

I was helped by the fact that it had become clearer to the people of Wales over the years that their government's ambitions were limited more by the nature of its powers than by its ambition. Rhodri Morgan, who had stood down as First Minister in 2009, was asked to take on the chair of a new 'Yes for Wales' campaign arguing for primary law-making powers. He did, with his usual enthusiasm and non-partisan engagement. A second referendum of the people of Wales was held in March 2011, prior to the election, to ask if the Assembly should now have primary law-making powers. A resounding level of supporters said yes – 65 per cent. Rhodri and all those of us who had campaigned for it were over the moon. Primary powers in the areas for which the Welsh Government had responsibility were therefore granted. We were on our way to becoming a parliament.

Now all I had to do was get Welsh Labour political support for my proposal! This was particularly important as I'd already announced that I would stand down from politics in 2011. I am a strong believer in the idea of constantly refreshing politicians, particularly in a small country. I'd therefore written publicly about the idea of a maximum term of office being no more than three Assembly terms. On that basis I'd announced my own retirement from politics two years previously, with an intention to live as lightly on the planet as I could while continuing to advocate the sustainability agenda to anyone who would listen. I needed therefore to get the proposition both into the Labour Party Manifesto for the next Assembly election and – if Labour was successful – into the Programme for Government, the legislative programme.

What I proposed and what went into the manifesto was to deliver on 'One Wales, One Planet' and its vision of a sustainable Wales.

To reflect this Welsh Labour in government will:

Maintain our commitment to the Sustainable Development Scheme
– One Wales One Planet – that sets out how Welsh Labour
in Government will use its devolved powers – from health,
transport to education – to make all our public services sustain-
able and reduce Wales' environmental impact on the world.
Legislate to embed sustainable development as the central
organising principle in all our actions across government and
all public bodies.

Visioning

*Legislate to put in place a new independent sustainable develop-
ment body for Wales, following the Tory-led U.K. Government's
decision to scrap the Sustainable Development Commission.*

The great thing about living in a small country with manifesto-led
government was that once this was agreed and in the manifesto as I
proposed, I could be confident it would happen (provided Labour was
in government in the fourth Assembly – and provided it also went
into the Programme for Government). Since the referendum had now
given the incoming Welsh Government primary powers for the first
time, Wales was ready for a fresh approach to institutional change.
When Labour won the election, the opportunity was immediately
created for the vision for 'One Wales, One Planet' (outlined in full in
appendix 1) to be translated into what has now become the Well-being
of Future Generations (Wales) Act 2015.

'John Clare, in his poem *The Nightingale's Nest*, reminds us that *nature is the builder, and contrives Homes for her children's comfort*. Will their understanding of nature be better than ours? Their use of language will tell us. So my take is as follows: successful delivery of the WFG Act will mean that the words of nature – words like 'Dandelion', 'Otter', 'Bramble', 'Acorn', and 'Conker' – will once again be part of the everyday language of children, and be reflected in the way they live their lives as adults.'

Simon Bilsborough, civil servant,
co-author of 'One Wales, One Planet', 2009

'The Act is also explicitly designed as a tool for continuously challenging business as usual.'

Michael Palmer, formerly of the Wales Audit Office,
now Fellow at the Institute for Advanced Sustainability Studies
at Potsdam University

CHAPTER 3

Networking

The Act and Its Delivery in Wales, 2011–2015

*A network is non-hierarchical. It is a web of connections
among equals, held together not by force, obligation,
material incentive, or social contract, but by shared values
and the understanding that some tasks can be accomplished
together that could never be accomplished separately.*

DONELLA MEADOWS

In May 2011 I made a deliberate choice to 'walk off my old life into my new' by re-walking the Pembrokeshire Coast Path 40 years on and reconnecting with nature. Wherever you start your journey on the coast in Wales, be prepared for an instant assault on your senses. Each day brought changing rock formations and soaring birds – razorbills and guillemots, herons and cormorants – and the flowers, bluebells, foxgloves, burdock, pyramid orchids, thrift and tiny sea pinks, speedwell, egg and bacon squills. We foraged for samphire and wild sorrel, remarking on the shining abundance of blackberries yet to come later in the year. We swam in pools, in surf, with seals, in the rain or magically in the light of the setting sun, showering under waterfalls. It's always hard to find the words to describe the rocks, the cliffs, the arches, the mossy caves, the bridges you see on your way. The coastline shows off nature at her most imaginative while also demonstrating evidence of long human occupation with distinctive Iron Age hill forts guarding promontories along the way, but it is the contrasts that make the walk so wonderful. Red sandstone streaked with algae in one place; black sheer jagged limestone cliffs and toothlike rock formations in another. In the hub of the energy industry in Wales, we saw campions, maids of honour, cornflowers, bluebells and lots of others I couldn't name, a swan nesting, and a family of jays too young to fly. Further north, the coast path hugs the edges of cliffs so tightly that mile after mile you experience sheer plunges and fantastic rock formations and caves demonstrating coastal erosion in action.

How do we describe nature if we don't have the words? The words I've used here have grown with me since childhood over a lifetime of reading and observing; they are comfortable friends seducing me with their accuracy of description, enabling me to make sense of the world. How do you describe blackberries or bluebells or moss without the words? The *Oxford Junior Dictionary* has removed all three words – 'moss,' 'blackberry' and 'bluebell' – and replaced them with new words in common currency among children: 'blog', 'chatroom', 'database'. Words already gone from the dictionary include 'acorn', 'adder', 'bramble', 'conker'. The dictionary compilers justified their actions in 2015 by saying, 'All our dictionaries are designed to reflect language as it is used, rather than seeking to prescribe certain words or certain usages.' Children's understanding of nature is being silenced by adults who should know better. My generation's natural pleasures – blackberry picking; playing conkers; the awesome sight of a knot of adders I once witnessed on the sunlit hillside above my home – are now wordless. If I asked the meaning of a word as a child, I would be sent to the dictionary so I could find out the meaning myself and then asked to apply it in a sentence so I would remember it. Perhaps that's why I became an English teacher! There is something quite disturbing about a dictionary – particularly a well-respected dictionary – helping children navigate a virtual world rather than help them recognise the species losses on their doorstep in the real one.

Coming together:
how the Act came into being

The forging of the Well-being of Future Generations (Wales) Act was a uniquely Welsh collaborative project in which thousands of people of all ages participated, moving the focus from duty to action and delivery. In this chapter I celebrate the networking that nurtured the Act into life and into law, to deliver on the vision of 'One Wales, One Planet'. I will outline the mechanisms for delivery, including the establishment and role of the Future Generations Commissioner, how the Act is monitored and the opportunity for the new act to be the mechanism at the heart of government to change governance, policy and delivery behaviour.

A legal duty in respect of sustainable development duty may act as a powerful educator of all actors in society and in focusing action in government in particular.
VICTORIA JENKINS, Hillary Rodham Clinton School of Law,
Swansea University, 2002

New beginnings – and an ending: 2011

The fourth Welsh general election took place on 5 May 2011. It was a strange time. Although I had chosen to stand down from my safe Labour seat, the Labour Party had been my life and my second family for 20 years. Many of my closest friends were in politics; my family and I lived and breathed politics, and most people could not understand why I'd chosen to leave it. I loved representing Pontypridd and its diverse mix of inhabitants; being close to the capital city and the gateway to the valleys, I had the most literate ward in Wales in my constituency along with the least literate – a stone's throw apart. So unusual was it for a politician to voluntarily give up the gravy train, I was asked by the press if I was pregnant (too old) or whether there was some family scandal about to break (too boring) or whether I was ill ('don't want to intrude'), but the truth was much more mundane.

71

I'd been privileged to carry out the only two ministerial jobs I wanted to do – Education, Lifelong Learning and Skills, and Environment, Sustainability and Housing. I firmly believed then – and still do now – that in a small country, there should be a maximum number of terms for which someone can stand for political office. I felt that three terms (four years each at the time) was the right balance for me, and therefore I stood down on this basis. Of course, I had regrets about leaving a world I loved, not least the adrenalin-pumping existence of being a minister at the heart of Welsh political action, but I have never had any regrets about the decision I made. Longevity of political representation can lead to the complacency of incumbency. Politicians lead a very privileged existence compared with most of the population of Wales; a set maximum term in my view would help design out bad behaviour and reinforce good behaviour.

I still treasure the Labour Party Manifesto for the 2011 Welsh general election. It was important on so many levels. Following the successful outcome of the Welsh referendum earlier that year, this was the first manifesto that enabled the Labour Party to propose new primary legislation to the people of Wales – and what radical laws were proposed: the commitment to make sustainable development the central principle, to live within our environmental limits and also to fundamentally change the process of human organ donation to one of presumed consent. Here once again was Wales' innovation in action – but now it could be legislatively delivered, whereas previously, despite Wales having been the first nation in the U.K. to propose the banning of smoking in public places, it had not had the powers at that time to turn policy into law. Previous key innovations had been policy ones – free prescriptions for all in light of the number of people on low incomes with chronic health problems; free bus passes for the over-60s to encourage greater use of public transport. As policies, they could be dispensed with immediately by any incoming administration; now proposals could be put into law to explicitly endure for current and future generations, and key amongst them was my proposal. How good was that as an exit card from politics?

Networking

When asked why I wasn't prepared to change my mind and stay on, in light of the radical nature of what I was proposing, I also thought it was really important that I was not the one to deliver the new legislation. I'd become too closely identified with the sustainability agenda as the champion of sustainability for the Welsh Government in the cabinet and to the wider world. If any issue was raised with a sustainability query, it came to me. If anyone had to appear publicly to talk about sustainability, it was always me. I was in danger of being the only sustainability voice in the government, when the very thing I was trying to achieve was to make us all guardians of a more sustainable future; responsible stewards of our precious inheritance.

The groundbreaking legislation we have now is an articulation of 'One Wales, One Planet' into law, but a law that was influenced enormously by people outside government. I want to pay a huge tribute to the 30 civil society members of the Sustainable Development Alliance – particularly WWF, Oxfam, Friends of the Earth and the international development organisations – who worked tirelessly with government and opposition parties to influence the collective inputs of subsequent ministers, each of whom added something valuable into the process. I am confident that the legislation is better for my leaving it to others – while still being available for the occasional phone call or meeting to return to first principles when necessary.

In the period after the results of the election were known, but before the new government was formally confirmed, I was invited by a senior civil servant, Matthew Quinn, Director of Environment, to privately address civil servants on my expectations of what the new law would expect from them. This was a really interesting request! The fact that Wales had now acquired primary powers had transformed their roles overnight; most had never created legislation – and of course no-one anywhere had created *this* legislation! About a hundred people attended, in person or remotely. They were excited, deadpan, dismissive in pretty well equal measures as I took them through the history and the opportunity for Wales to lead the way. Who would not want to work for a government forging a path for future generations? I asked. What was on their minds then, and remains an important theme even now, was the question of how committed the new government would really be to this. Would it be the first piece of legislation (as I hoped) or would its novel nature mean that it would come later in the Programme for Government? Or, said one, who accused me of leaving a bomb for the incoming administration and then walking away: now that I'd gone, 'would it be in the Programme at all?' Of course, I was a little concerned about this too, but I was not really worried, as I knew cabinet colleagues who supported the principle, like me, were coming to the conclusion that the proposed law would give the civil service the delivery framework that had been previously lacking.

The argument for legislation

I think we all left the meeting considering the new powers to be a watershed moment for Wales. Law is different to policy. Policies can be changed in an instant; laws are more enduring and explicitly created to live longer than the governments that create them. Law therefore has a firmer intention behind it and requires a delivery mechanism that will satisfy a court. This meeting had been held because moving from policy to law is a significant change – with a significant workload attached. Although ministers set direction, it is the civil servants who have to craft the outcome.

For me, reflecting afterwards on the meeting, my key immediate priority was to make absolutely sure that my proposed law would go into the legislative Programme for Government, without which it couldn't be made at all! Talking to Carwyn Jones about this after the event was interesting. He was very conscious of the impact of the 2008 economic crash as the 2011 Assembly election approached, and that 'sustainability had slipped down the agenda as people worried about their jobs and finances. The need to live sustainably hadn't disappeared though and we wanted to ensure that it was included in the 2011 Programme for Government. It needed a bold step, beyond another policy document, so we took the decision to include a bill which would look at embedding long-term thinking into the work of government.'

This was not the first time legislation had been proposed, either – although it would be the first time that it would be delivered. Victoria Jenkins, lecturer in law at Swansea University, sent me a paper she'd written in 2002, evaluating the then-current mechanisms. Her conclusion was: 'If the government is truly committed to the achievement of sustainable development, it must recognise that it can only be achieved it it is accepted as its primary aim' and therefore there must be 'an overriding primary statutory duty for all public bodies to "contribute to the achievement of sustainable development".'

This was a goosebumps moment. Here was someone I'd never met with a completely different skill set articulating a proposition similar to mine – and who had beaten me to it by nearly a decade. She was arguing from the evidence of the lack of consistency in the application of the sustainable development duties in the U.K.; I was arguing from the basis that what is statutory has a greater chance of getting done. Both of us were arguing from a place of conviction that this was an important and necessary change to put at the heart of the framework of government.

The second academic legal contribution came from Andrea Ross from the Dundee University School of Law. In 2010 she had evaluated the existing legislative models in Wales, Canada and Scotland, concluding that, while legislation that adopts the Sustainable Development Commission's vision of sustainable development as the central organising principle of governance in the U.K. is 'desperately needed and arguably is the only way forward, it may take the U.K. administrations a while to be willing to give this legislative backing. It will likely take the courts longer still.' This was a prescient observation which we discussed personally, as I was keen to understand the legal as well as the political challenges. In politics it is easy to commit verbally – say, to a climate emergency – but somebody then has to go away and translate that into regulation, policy and action. When you are leading the pack with an idea, good practice is not always easily available!

Courts require case law and precedents to establish meaning, and a single piece of legislation does not on its own establish that.

The third key legal input, specific to the new Welsh opportunity, came from Peter Roderick, a public interest environmental barrister, legal adviser to Friends of the Earth and co-director of the Climate Justice Programme. Peter was commissioned by WWF to articulate what an act delivering on the proposition I'd put forward in our manifesto might look like translated into law.

In his paper 'The National Assembly for Wales and Taking the Longer View', published in June 2011, he proposed an act with three limbs:

> *Firstly, requiring Welsh ministers to exercise their duties and powers in order to achieve sustainable development, to adopt a sustainable development strategy, to make sustainable development the central organising principle of government and by enacting the precautionary principle.*
> *Secondly, the Act should acknowledge the existence of environmental limits expressly, and Wales' need to keep within them, by starting to establish a system respecting planetary boundaries which would evolve over time.*
> *Thirdly, the Act should put the Commissioner for Sustainable Futures on a statutory footing as a strong and independent champion of the environment and future generations, with significant powers and duties.*

It's probably worth a short reflection on what might constitute success of the central organising principle, since this would occupy the lawmakers for some time. In 'One Wales, One Planet', we described sustainable development as a process on the way to achieving 'sustainability'. Such an interpretation recognises that what we consider sustainable now may not be considered so in the future as our understanding of the impact of our behaviour grows or shifts in society value different aspects of life. Therefore, for me, the journey must always be about exceeding the present good practice. Housing is a good metaphor here: so-called sustainable homes built in the 1980s are classed as inefficient now, because we are continually dialling up the standards of sustainability. This approach was used in the development of the new act.

The first milestone:
the Programme for Government

On 12 July 2011 the Programme for Government was published, which said:

> *There will be a Bill which aims to set Wales apart as a sustainable nation by:*
>
> *embedding sustainable development as the central organising*
> *principle in all actions across Government and all public bodies*
> *by providing for the establishment of a new independent body – to*
> *continue the legacy of the [U.K.] Sustainable Development Com-*
> *mission in a way that best reflects Welsh interests and needs*

In his introduction to Assembly Members, Carwyn Jones said, 'Sustainability lies at the heart of the Welsh Government's agenda for Wales and it lies too at the heart of this legislative programme.' This was when intention moved to action – when Wales intentionally broke away from the norms of unsustainable government behaviour – and not one commentator picked it up! This was a huge fundamental shift from promoting sustainable development as *one* of the imperatives driving government, to using sustainable development as *the* central organising principle against which other imperatives would be balanced.

The third Effectiveness Review
The legislative process did indeed start in the first year and then took three years and four ministers to go onto the statute book. But first

there was the Effectiveness Review of my scheme 'One Wales, One Planet' – this time delivered by PwC, one of the big global accountancy and management firms. This was particularly important as it was conducted in the explicit knowledge that the incoming Welsh Government planned to introduce legislation based on this scheme. The review commended the 2007–2011 government's 'strong political and organisational leadership' for setting 'a positive context for sustainable development in Wales'; in particular by enshrining the legislative commitment and maintaining the independent challenge by the appointment of a Sustainable Futures Commissioner, despite the U.K. Government's decision to disband the Sustainable Development Commission. It commended the way we had engaged positively with our external stakeholders and noted our Sustainable Development Charter, which by then had been signed by over 100 organisations and through which we had set up a network of organisations to share learning and best practice on sustainable development. It also commended the government's own internal environmental performance, our 'silo-busting' (cross-portfolio) household energy and Climate Change Commission work. This was the most positive review to date, and my hope was that putting the commitment into a new law would provide the effective, systemic, coordinating mechanism that was still identified as lacking. Without addressing this, PwC said, it would be hard for the Welsh Government to be an exemplar and bring others to the table.

The making of the Act: 2012–2015

The First Minister charged with delivering the new commitment was my old friend and walking partner John Griffiths AM, now my successor as Minister for Environment and Sustainable Development. He was the minister who got the ball rolling by publishing a green paper at the end of 2011 to test the appetite of public sector partners for the terms of engagement. He told me, 'When I became minister for the environment in 2011, the proposed legislation was causing a considerable amount of head scratching among ministers and civil service alike. At numerous meetings there was difficulty in achieving clarity as to how legislation could be written to ensure a practical step change in action on the ground. An act would have symbolic importance but also had to bite on delivery of policy and services.'

The nature of duty?

Key questions included the definition of sustainable development and the nature of the duty to be imposed. Should it be a duty to produce a strategy, or a duty to comply, or a duty to have regard, or a duty to assess decision making, and so on? What should be in the legislation and therefore enduring, and what should be in regulations and therefore changeable? How should compliance be measured? What decisions should it affect? At what level should the duty operate? What should the new sustainable development body look like?

The responses to these questions led to the white paper 'Proposals for a Sustainable Development Bill' published in May 2012, in the same year that world governments met for Rio +20 in Rio de Janeiro, 20 years after the original Earth Summit that had proposed Agenda 21. The white paper proposed a duty that:

- Applies to higher-level decisions adopted by organisations delivering public services to guide the way they work.
- Ensures that those decisions have to be informed by key sustainable development factors.
- Requires organisations to report on how they have complied with the duty through their existing annual reporting.

Bringing in expertise (and scrutiny) from outside the government

Civil society in Wales, as represented by all the key voluntary organisations and umbrella groupings, from the outset was very supportive of the direction of travel, describing the white paper as an 'amazing opportunity to put global social justice and environmental protection at the heart of the Government of Wales' but also calling for specific strong measures in the bill to ensure that the new duty to deliver should:

Clearly define sustainable development.

Require Welsh Government ministers and the devolved public sector to exercise their duties and powers to achieve sustainable development, both within Wales and with regard to the impacts internationally.

Be supplemented by a national strategy (or strategies) to lead to clear actions to:

- *Drive down carbon and other greenhouse gas emissions.*
- *Create and sustain green jobs.*
- *Promote ethical, Fairtrade and sustainable procurement by the public sector.*
- *Drive sustainable and ethical action by businesses that are supported by Welsh Government in relation to their activities domestically and internationally.*

Explicitly recognise and give regard to the international impacts of Wales – for example, the supply chains of the Welsh public and private sectors – in terms of carbons intensity, food security, et cetera; as well as the activities of Welsh businesses abroad and the carbon emissions produced in Wales.

Since environmental catastrophes and species loss were becoming more noticeable with each passing year, charities dedicated to environmental action – WWF, Friends of the Earth and the Wildlife Trusts – strongly supported the definition in 'One Wales, One Planet' with reference to 'using only our fair share of the Earth's resources' and offered to develop specific wording to make this clear in law. Right from the beginning, therefore, the influence of civil society expertise is clear on the development of what was to become the core of the

Well-being of Future Generations Act. WWF convened and supported 30 key civil society organisations into the Sustainable Development Alliance, of which I was a member, which kept ministers and civil servants on their toes to ensure the legislation was meaningful and robust, sometimes with a gentle nudge, sometimes with a well-argued, forceful challenge in order to influence the formal government-led reference group.

Connecting environmental justice and social justice into a sustainable society

As the proposals for the bill developed, voices inside and outside government argued that there was too strong an environmental focus to the bill, which needed rebalancing with a societal focus. It still seems odd to me that since humans obviously have to live within our environmental limits (as we only have one planet available to us), taking action to do so is seen as environmental rather than societal. As a green socialist, I would argue if we want to create better opportunities for the future of humanity – and indeed other species – then the foundation of our future well-being must be to look after nature a great deal better than we do – which is why it was so important to me to explicitly include this in the law. I would suggest this will become more of a battleground in the future if our environment, and therefore our life chances, continues to degrade without appropriate intervention. The UN view of the environment is as a fundamental foundation. We should be adopting this approach.

In the next cabinet reshuffle, the First Minister, Carwyn Jones, moved the portfolio responsibility to a new minister: Huw Lewis, Minister for Communities and Tackling Poverty. This was an explicit move to highlight the importance of social justice as a key sustainability issue, an issue at the heart of Welsh Government concerns, and, I was told confidentially, to keep the agenda alive. Huw was a powerful advocate for young people and for their voice to be heard, and like me, he was a teacher by profession. He had been my 'twin' at the beginning of the National Assembly, when his constituency of Merthyr and mine had been twinned to create a balanced male and female slate of Labour candidates. His tenure in this responsibility was only a matter of months – but they were a very important few months as he questioned the very name of the Sustainable Development Bill on the basis that it would mean nothing to his constituents in one of the poorest districts in Wales. It was this questioning that led to the agenda being retitled Future Generations.

The third minister who assumed responsibility, Jeff Cuthbert, was the incoming Minister for Communities and Tackling Poverty. Jeff was an affable minister who had particularly strong cross-party and community credentials. He had founded and chaired the Cross-Party Built Environment Group, the Cross-Party Healthy Living Group, the Cross-Party Diabetes Group and also co-founded and co-chaired the Cross-Party Beer and Pub Group! Jeff told me a few months ago: 'When responsibility for the bill was handed to me by Carwyn Jones, I was apprehensive. Not because I couldn't see the importance of the vision but because the focus of the bill was seen as heavily on the side of conservation of the environment. I wanted to move the whole mission to embrace the notion of sustainable jobs and training, cohesive communities, culture and the Welsh language as well as responsibility for maintaining our natural environment.'

He felt strongly that if you cannot give hope to people that their livelihood, and that of their children and grandchildren, is of paramount importance to government, it would be more difficult getting them to make their natural environment a key priority. He remembered 'battling' with representatives of environmental groups on these issues, who feared that this broader approach meant that Welsh Government was watering down its commitment to the environment. He hoped that 'ultimately we managed to convince them that our broader approach was correct and did not represent any reduction in our enthusiasm for safeguarding the natural environment'.

Two other important inputs were made under Jeff's time in office. The first was to create new statutory Public Services Boards so all public sector partners would be required to work collaboratively for sustainable outcomes. Of course, as executive agencies of government, this requirement could take many forms, including potentially withholding government funding or setting conditions for its use.

The second was fundamental to the direction of travel for the bill. Jeff and his officials realised that the government needed to convince what might be a sceptical public in Wales that this new law was the right thing to do. He therefore launched 'The Wales We Want', a national conversation with Welsh people and communities.

'The Wales We Want'

Jeff charged Peter Davies, the Sustainable Futures Commissioner, with the responsibility to lead a year-long conversation with people across Wales, supported by Cynnal Cymru and involving thousands of people through public forums and social media. During this lengthy process, the Welsh Government drew heavily on international evidence, models and experience, not least the contemporaneous process 'The World We Want' under way through the United Nations to replace the Millennium Development Goals (2000–2015) with the Sustainable Development Goals (2015–2030).

The title, 'The Wales We Want', reflected the UN's ongoing 'World We Want' conversation. Through the conversation, people were asked about the Wales they wanted to leave behind for their children and grandchildren, and to consider the challenges, aspirations and ways to solve long-term problems to create the Wales they want by 2050. Given that the focus was on future generations, there were hundreds of events across Wales, including schools, colleges, youth forums and more specific groups such as young farmers and Urdd Gobaith Cymru – the Welsh-language youth movement. The local conversations directly reflected the vision in 'One Wales, One Planet' and introduced the idea that this was about creating a new vision for Wales that government could legislate for, but required much wider public engagement in delivery – in other words, a duty that bound government but also extended beyond it to apply across the wider public sector as I'd initially proposed.

'The Wales We Want' was preceded by a national launch in the Millennium Centre in Cardiff Bay at which Michael Sheen, Unicef U.K. ambassador, actor and proud son of Port Talbot, spoke passionately about his commitment to the Wales that he wanted to pass on to the next generation and beyond. He talked about the loss of the youth-theatre opportunity that had created his own acting career and called on such opportunities to be reintroduced. His support and intervention had a very positive effect galvanising people across Wales. A network of Futures Champions was established, representing different geographic communities and communities of interest. Michael hoped passionately that the Future Generations Bill would allow creative opportunities to the abundance of the Welsh talent that exists. He said: 'If there is truly a desire to understand the long-term issues of the people of Wales, then improving their lives and their children's, and their children's children, must be at the heart of this enterprise . . . Only then can we face the truth about ourselves and move forwards towards a culture of inclusivity and respect where each life feels important.'

'The Wales We Want' engaged with thousands of people across Wales, spawning sector interest groups such as 'The Wales Women Want', 'The Llanelli We Want', 'The Wales Carers Want', 'The Energy We Want', 'The Wales Young Farmers Want', all debating what they wanted their futures to look like. Futures Champions came from grassroots organisations and raised issues in their locality. Pupils at Ysgol David Hughes on the island of Anglesey, for example, wanted a Wales where 'Welsh language has increased status and more speakers; we are an example of a country fuelled sustainably and fully carbon neutral; our history and heritage are preserved; the community works together to look after the area; everyone is treated equally and everyone has opportunity to achieve their potential; we are in control and closer to independence; young people can voice their opinions and be listened to'.

Networking

What was interesting about this process is the gap it highlighted between the people's views of what we should value and protect and what we have failed to value enough and whether the bill would now enable Wales to revalue it. At the time the bill was published, 'The Wales We Want' conversations had climate change as by far the single most critical issue, closely followed by environment, employment, education and health – yet at the time, the government did not have climate change as its top priority. People valued local leisure facilities, parks and libraries, yet these were in danger of being sold off by local government, often without real consultation, in times of austerity. I once said to someone who asked me what success under the Act would look like that it would be when the community facilities people rely upon heavily – the leisure centres, the libraries, the swimming pools, the community halls – would be the last to be sold off, not the first.

'The Wales We Want Report: A Report on Behalf of Future Generations' identified seven foundations for the well-being of future generations:

1. Children need to be given the best start in life from very early years.
2. Future generations need thriving communities built on a strong sense of place.
3. Living within global environmental limits, managing our resources efficiently and valuing our environment are critical.
4. Investing in growing our local economy is essential for the well-being of future generations.
5. The well-being of all depends on reducing inequality and a greater value on diversity.
6. Greater engagement in the democratic process, a stronger citizen voice and active participation in decision making are fundamental to the well-being of future generations.
7. Celebrating success, valuing our heritage, culture and language will strengthen our identity for future generations.

These foundations influenced the final iterations of the bill before it became law. Through the conversations, a number of ways to build a movement across different age groups and sectors in Wales were proposed: for example, by actively working with Futures Champions, early adopters, town and community councils and the new collaborative Public Services Boards. Shaping the indicator set that will measure progress against the goals was seen as particularly important.

Moving from 'seeking' to 'ensuring'

The bill as initially drafted was a cautious attempt by the government lawyers to capture the manifesto commitment to 'Legislate to embed sustainable development as the central organising principle in all our actions across government and all public bodies by using words like "seek to ensure" and "seek to achieve".' I was pleased to see that the core elements at the heart of the legislation were those I'd proposed, and that civil society had proposed. What we (civil society and I) needed to do was to turn 'seek to ensure' into a requirement to deliver, otherwise the new duty, despite all the effort, would potentially be less robust than the original duty. There was a shaky moment or two with a number of senior political and civil service voices arguing that the previous duty was sufficient anyway; some voices were raised to 'bin the bill', a mixture of those who did not support the agenda anyway and those who had been its biggest supporters, but who now felt that the bill was not sufficiently robust on matters such as climate change, environmental limits and the precautionary principle.

I was invited into government to meet with ministers and special advisers to articulate what I'd originally envisaged and why, which was the need to legislate to enshrine the central organising principle to create a clear and level playing field. Interestingly, although there were tensions in government about being held to account in that way, by this point the appetite for the bill as 'permission to think differently' was growing through 'The Wales We Want'. The government held firm on its manifesto commitment. The bill was changed and strengthened through its legislative process, largely by the expert inputs from the alliance.

Halfway through this process, there was another cabinet reshuffle. The fourth minister to take on the responsibility was Carl Sargeant, Minister for Natural Resources, who saw the bill through into law. Bringing it back to an environment portfolio at this time was important as the search for balance between environmental and social domains of well-being rumbled on. The environment sector had argued that the bill 'does not treat the three pillars of sustainable development equally: it is much more focused on the social pillar and is more of a public sector reform bill than a sustainable development one'. In the bill's stage 2, therefore, amendments making direct references to 'climate change' were inserted into two goals and other goals were amended to include a more explicit reference to the concept of environmental limits in the context of a resilient environment.

During stage 3 proceedings, the definition of sustainable development was included with a stronger requirement to carry it out. During this intense process, WWF was absolutely critical. It commissioned legal views from academics and lawyers, including a queen's counsel, to provide workable solutions for issues which government lawyers had claimed could not be solved. With this advice in hand, WWF was able to ask for specific amendments to virtually every clause in part 1 of the bill, with most aimed at tightening the language and making the duties bite. They also fought to get sufficient powers for the Future Generations Commissioner and are still today arguing for greater powers of redress.

In one sense you could say that this is a normal story of legislative development, even if the legislation itself is unusual. The key factors that led to the Act we have now include the facts that the government had a very small majority, so it had to work closely with other political parties to achieve a cross-party consensus to take the legislation through; that civil society through the expert Sustainable Development Alliance was geared up, well informed, well researched, legally armed (and therefore dangerous) and very effective in arguing its position and getting support for that position; that the Sustainable Futures Commissioner was passionate about community engagement and put in the time and effort to ensure that 'The Wales We Want' conversation was a success; and that there was an excellent team of civil servants who wanted the Act to deliver what has been identified time and time again through effectiveness reviews – the effective mechanism to drive the sustainable development agenda across the civil service.

The Well-being of Future Generations (Wales) Act as passed is a framework for action at the heart of government, a context for all government activity. What the government then needed to do was to create more traditional compliance legislation to underpin the behaviour change it sought to encourage. Carl Sargeant drove through the first piece of companion legislation, the Environment Act, which makes the sustainable management of natural resources a legal duty. This makes Wales one of the few countries globally which has taken such a strong approach, one of the first countries to fully legislate for the UN Convention on Biological Diversity, and one of the first states or regions to legislate for carbon budgets. This is essential to ensure our children and grandchildren will have access to the resources they need, such as fresh water, adequate food and enjoyment of nature. Notably too it is only in Wales that the Brundtland definition of 1987 has been translated into law, despite its being the most common definition of sustainable development in the world.

What was worth celebrating at the point the bill became an act, in April 2015, was the number of people who contributed to its development. Wales is a small country, yet thousands of people had engaged with the process, with realistic proposals to improve their villages, towns, cities, their communities, their environment. What a gift to a government wanting to serve future generations! Each minister had contributed a different characteristic reflecting the breadth of the vision; the political parties in the National Assembly, civil society, the Sustainable Futures Commissioner and 'The Wales We Want' conversations all contributed something significant. It is truly an act made in Wales, by Wales for Wales.

The Well-being of Future Generations (Wales) Act 2015

So here we are in April 2015 when the National Assembly of Wales passed the first act in the world to look after the interests of future generations. You will see from the comments above, and many more throughout this book, how excited the passing of such an act has made others. Unfortunately, it's much more difficult to know how to make the Act itself exciting to the reader, unless you have also spent years fighting for your government to make decisions in a more sensible way, having regard to current and future generations. Stories are always going to be much more interesting than legislation, but because the message of this story so far is that legislation is essential to change behaviour, for me the Act is about as exciting as it gets! I do want to pay tribute to the government for the large number of provisions in the Act which address the issues raised in previous effectiveness reviews. These are the necessary nuts and bolts by which the Commissioner and the Auditor General in particular can hold the government and the public services to account. If you want a detailed look at the provisions, the link to the Welsh Government's short guide to the Act is included among the links to key documents in the "2016–Present: Implenting the Act" section of appendix 2, on page 191. What I've highlighted below are those transformational provisions which seem to excite people most when I'm explaining the Act to them for the first time.

The Act

Defines the sustainable development principle in line with the 1987 Brundtland Report definition as seeking 'to ensure that the needs of the present are met without compromising the ability of future generations to meet their own needs'.

#futuregen

Defines sustainable development as 'the process of improving the economic, social, environmental and cultural well-being of Wales' by taking action, in accordance with the sustainable development principle, with the aim of achieving the well-being goals.

Introduces seven statutory 'well-being goals', with legal descriptions of their meaning. In brief, the goals are: a prosperous Wales; a resilient Wales; a healthier Wales; a more equal Wales; a Wales of cohesive communities; a Wales of vibrant culture and thriving Welsh language; and a globally responsible Wales.

Introduces five specified ways of working, namely, to adopt a long-term perspective, take an integrated approach, involve citizens, collaborate and pursue a preventive approach.

Places a legal obligation on all public bodies in the responsibility of the Welsh Government to 'carry out sustainable development', including a requirement to set and publish 'well-being objectives', to take 'all reasonable steps' to meet those objectives, and to report on progress annually.

Creates an independent Future Generations Commissioner with responsibilities to:

- Act as a guardian of the ability of future generations to meet their needs.
- Monitor and assess the extent to which well-being objectives set by public bodies are being met.
- Publish periodically a report on how public bodies can improve the way they pursue their well-being objectives and give expression to the principle of sustainable development.
- Advise, encourage and promote action towards meeting well-being objectives.
- Carry out research into the delivery of the goals, indicators, milestones and sustainable development principle.
- Make recommendations to public bodies – which public bodies must take 'all reasonable steps' to follow.

Networking

I've said previously that one of the biggest challenges is to persuade economic and finance ministers – and their civil servants – to move away from more traditional policies. For me, the single most exciting provision in the Act is the redefining of prosperity in one of the seven goals which along with the five ways of working are at the core of the legislation.

The Act redefines a prosperous Wales as an 'innovative, productive and low-carbon society which recognises the limits of the global environment and therefore uses resources efficiently and proportionately, including acting on climate change, and which develops a skilled and well-educated population in an economy which generates wealth and provides employment opportunities, allowing people to take advantage of the wealth generated through securing decent work'. So here we have in law a requirement to deliver a low-carbon economy operating within environmental limits, tackling climate change, upskilling the population to take advantage of decent work. This is a well-being economics agenda for a country which led the industrial revolution. Now, that is exciting!

Perhaps I should leave the last word on the provisions of the Act to Professor Jonathan Boston, from the Institute for Governance and Policy Studies at Victoria University of Wellington, who was commissioned by the New Zealand Government to evaluate how to enhance long-term governance through better parliamentary scrutiny. In his report *Foresight, Insight and Oversight,* he describes the Act as:

> *comprehensive, ambitious and demanding. It is the first legislation of its kind anywhere in the world. It imposes significant new obligations on public bodies with respect to not only their overall goals but also their ways of working. It establishes a detailed framework for setting national indicators, objectives and goals, assessing trends, monitoring performance and holding ministers and public bodies to account. It has considerable potential, given time, to reframe the mind-sets and strategies of governmental decision-makers and public institutions, modify intertemporal preferences, alter*

budgetary priorities and change how public bodies conduct their activities and engage with citizens and other stakeholders.

The role of the Future Generations Commissioner for Wales

One of the key areas of discussion in the development of the Act was in relation to the role, powers and authority of the new Future Generations Commissioner. Wales has been innovative in the establishment of independent commissioners, from leading the way in the U.K. in the creation of the first Children's Commissioner in 2001 to the first Older People's Commissioner in the U.K. in 2008, the Welsh-language Commissioner in 2012 and a Future Generations Commissioner in 2015.

The Well-being of Future Generations Act both inspires and joins international voices in three important ways. It encourages thinking in systems, making visible the connections and dependencies between policy 'silos'; it expands planning horizons, bringing the unheard voices of future generations into the present; it questions what we value and measure, from moribund and arbitrary economic measures like GDP [gross domestic product], and promotes things that really matter to citizens and communities.

SUE PRITCHARD, director, RSA Food, Farming and Countryside Commission (and Welsh farmer)

Each commissioner is independent of government – and indeed all have been very challenging to government – but they are ultimately government appointments informed by their sectors and the legislature. As Jonathan Boston says, 'From an international perspective, the Office of the Future Generations Commissioner and the legislative context within which the Office operates are both unique. No identical – or even broadly equivalent – institution exists elsewhere.'

There was substantial debate over the establishment of the Commissioner role from early in the Act's development. Should it be a commission (a group of people who meet regularly without an office or wider role) or a commissioner (with an office and staff)? What should be the powers of a commissioner in a democracy? What powers are legitimate for a commissioner who is appointed by government, to have over others, such as public services officials and appointees, or democratically elected others, like elected local authority members?

What should the powers for intervention be? What should be the balance between 'critical friend' functions and 'holding to account' functions?

In the Act as passed, the Commissioner's main power lies in the capacity to 'name and shame' public bodies – including the Welsh Government – which must take all 'reasonable' steps to follow the Commissioner's recommendations. But in the end, public bodies are not obliged to follow what the Commissioner proposes unless compelled to do so by the government. Civil society fought hard for a robust right of enquiry – called 'power of review' in the Act. This was so the Commissioner could investigate systemic problems and require information from named public bodies for that purpose. At the moment, this is not in place, but this discussion will remain live and be influenced by events that may not have been envisaged yet. It is certainly true to say that there is cautionary advice here as two previous commissioner models in Hungary and Israel did not survive their making decisions unpopular with their democratically elected governments.

The first Future Generations Commissioner for Wales is Sophie Howe. Coming from a social justice background in equality and human rights and having been a Deputy Police Commissioner and the special adviser who supported the minister in taking the Act through to Royal Assent, she was an eminently sensible appointment for the first Commissioner, not least for her personal passion for sustainability.

Since her appointment, her aim has been to help the policy community understand the requirements and implications of the

Well-being Act, embed the principle of sustainable development in core governmental procedures and processes, reframe the nature of policy debate on key long-term issues and serve as a catalyst for change – in relation to both the substance of public policy and the processes of decision making.

This year – 2020 – five years after the Act was first passed, Sophie will publish her first statutory Future Generations Report, a year ahead of the next National Assembly for Wales election. This will contain her assessment of the improvements Welsh Government and public bodies should make to achieve the well-being goals as required by the Act. Her key recommendations from that report can be found in the 'The Last Word' at the end of this book.

Paying tribute to our passionate, energetic and committed civil society

What I noticed even more clearly once outside government was what a fantastic resource civil society in Wales is. The Well-being Act was not for them a piece of legislation; it was the chance to redefine Wales as a sustainable nation, delivering a vision crafted not just by politicians but also by its people – by Wales for Wales. Many voices contributed to the 'Wales We Want' national conversation and therefore to developing the Well-being Act – and many voices are still contributing now on what their hopes of the legislation are, aiming to galvanise government and the public sector to be the best they can. There is passion and drive galore, some still waiting to be harnessed. When I was commissioned to write this book, I decided to ask for the widest possible range of views to incorporate. I was deluged by contributors keen to celebrate the opportunity of the Act and to advise on how to improve its delivery, and it has been an absolute joy to know how much of an extraordinarily committed resource there is in Wales and beyond. I was not able to include all the voices in the book itself, but from here on you will hear excerpts from them, and their contributions in full are on my website www.janedavidson.wales.

Networking

I begin with the inspiring, inclusive vision of Dr Oliver Balch, sustainability journalist and researcher:

For the WFGA to be the best it can be requires it to escape the confines of government and policy-making. It needs to be owned by everyone. And by 'it', I mean the vision of a better, cleaner, happier, more prosperous Wales. What can be more exciting or hope-giving than that? A country that is fit for future generations is something that every citizen can unite around, something every community can pursue, something every school can pass on to its pupils. Instil that narrative in the heart of every citizen and the Act is already half-way delivered.

Anne Meikle, director at WWF Cymru, sets out a manifesto for change, of mindset, culture and accountability, reminding us that it is the responsibility not just of government but also the wider society to hold us to account.

As a first step, we must do no more harm to the environment.

The Act alone *cannot make this happen.*

This needs leadership – from all political parties and from others who have influence – business leaders, religious and community leaders.

Decision makers must feel confident that the people of Wales want this to happen, so we need to hear *their voices, including those usually excluded – the young, the marginalised.*

We also need to challenge those leaders who are doing the wrong thing – those who quietly lobby for everything to stay as it is now – because it suits their personal interests.

We need the law to help this challenge, to ensure consequences for those who will not take more care and make bold change.

We also need new law to guarantee citizens' rights to challenge decisions and have their case investigated by an independent watchdog with teeth.

#futuregen

It must become politically, economically and socially unacceptable to destroy our children's future through destroying their environment.

On changing the mindset of government, Dr Alan Netherwood from Netherwood Sustainable Futures reminds us that it must be more than platitude:

Successful delivery of the Act would see a public sector, Commissioner's office and government which focus, not on platitudes or process or general commitments to the future well-being of current citizens, but truly represents the interests of unborn generations through advocacy, governance and decision making.

George Marshall, founder of Climate Outreach, articulates how we must use our unique strengths and traditions to make a law that is truly for Wales:

There is no single narrative for sustainability: there are a multitude, tailored to each distinct culture, and validating the traditions found in every county that connect people to land and nature.

In 2012 the Welsh Assembly commissioned Climate Outreach and a team of 10 researchers to explore the exceptional connection that Welsh people have to landscape, community and their ancient language. From focus groups across Wales, we developed a bilingual toolkit of distinct Welsh narratives and images for sustainability and climate change to support the legislation. We even challenged the placeless United Nations 'sustainable' jargon and recommended alternatives drawn from the Welsh language that held real cultural resonance [see appendix 2]. This was the first national environmental narratives project of its kind and is now being replicated around the world. As we move forward it is essential that all governments follow this example, challenge technocratic policy language and adopt language that weaves sustainability into their national stories.

Networking

Looking to the future, Andy Middleton, chief exploration officer at TYF and previously deputy chair at Cynnal Cymru – Sustain Wales, paints a brave new world for us to set our course by:

How far could Wales go?

When change blossoms, a future might look like this:

Wales' food was reinvented to a re-localised 'Hippocratic' system where land use, food production and nutrition are managed for the health of current and future citizens. The adoption of an initial '25 per cent local' approach across Wales created nearly 20,000 new jobs and re-engaged younger people with working with food and land.

Education gives every child an unshakeable confidence in their ability to shape a better world, with skills and know-how. It took less than 10 years for Wales' young people to perform on par with their Nordic counterparts, proving that impact learning can connect hearts, minds and results.

Dramatic increases of active and reflective time spent in nature, scaled up across Wales, reduced cost of mental health support by over £700 million a year.

When government, business and third-sector work with ambition and set goals bold enough to match the scale of challenge ahead, the compass for change will be set. The Well-being of Future Generations Act is the planner that will make bold journeys possible.

One of the most exciting themes that civil society picks up is the opportunity to create a prosperous, low-carbon economy, creating new jobs and skills that enrich society without damaging the environment. First, here's Mari Arthur, director of Cynnal Cymru – Sustain Wales: 'An entrepreneurial culture can be built while developing an understanding of coming demands and new opportunities. A Foundational Economy approach to energy will harness the skills of local people that are trained and educated specifically for this demand.

In addition, while keeping skills, work and profits in the regions of Wales, we will eliminate fuel poverty, harnessing our natural resources for our own needs first and exporting excess to generate community-owned wealth.'

Rhodri Thomas, principal sustainability consultant at Cynnal Cymru – Sustain Wales, continues this theme: 'Under the Act, a new law should be introduced to compel a rigorous shadow economy in which the currency is Carbon or Eco-credits. This would allow individuals and organisations to trade on the basis of off-setting harm or being paid to do no harm while also uphold the principle of "polluter pays". It would reward low-impact lifestyles and penalise greedy lifestyles.'

Eifion Williams, CEO of Circular Economy Wales, relates this to his own hometown:

I was born in what was, for a short time at least, Wales' highest village. Bwlchgwyn in North Wales had been surpassed by Trefil in Blaenau Gwent; a council error as opposed to Hugh Grant climbing a hill with buckets of soil. One of Jane Davidson's legacies, the Well-being of Future Generations Act, was passed in the same year my village fell from the record books. The Act made me focus on less trivial losses in my village. I made a rough count of the shops, chapels and other community spaces that had existed when I was a child compared to now. It was a staggering drop from 28 to 3. Something was missing, not only from my community, but everybody's. What was needed obviously was a creative and radical re-think.

During Jane Davidson's tenure in Welsh Government, I was working on the Zero Waste goals she had set for Wales. Inspired, I set out to create new business models utilising 'waste'. For my village, perhaps its rejuvenation lay in a 'new take' on the Circular Economy. Within industry, circular economic thinking is gaining traction fast, but a community-based approach, involving many players, could be devised if we want to reduce commuting, food miles and wealth leakage from the places where we live.

> *The 'Circular Economy Plus+' model, being pioneered by Cir-*
> *cular Economy Wales, seeks to mould and channel the outputs of*
> *local business towards people's needs, community by community.*
> *Resilient communities are not only in control of their resources but*
> *also their food and energy systems and the wealth of course that all*
> *this activity generates.*

Eifion has put these plans into practice – I follow his story in chapter 4.

Conversations: the young voices

When I asked young people to tell me their views for this book, we see a clear focus on what they think is important. Becky Ricketts, president of the Students' Union from my own university, University of Wales Trinity Saint David, articulates a clarion call for education:

> *My question to you is this: why are we preparing our children for*
> *a world that may not be able to support life as we know it? If I*
> *were to have the power, my primary decision would be to include*
> *real climate education and education of the Act into our schools,*
> *colleges, universities and even workplaces – the Well-Being of our*
> *Future Generations depends on us all, and we have an obligation*
> *as a 'Globally Responsible Wales' to only positively contribute to*
> *this crisis.*

This theme is further developed by Chris Roscoe, One Young World delegate (Wales), who said: 'By empowering citizens with the skills of lifelong learning, and developing within them an openness to change, future generations will be equipped with the fundamental tools to address current and future challenges.'

Other key themes being played out for this generation are the importance of young voices in decision making, articulated so well by Joe Stockley, a young member of the board of the Wales Council for Voluntary Action: 'A more equal Wales demands genuine listening. A more equal Wales demands voices that aren't comfortable to hear. A more equal Wales demands more young people in decision making.' This call, effectively a 'don't make policy about us, without us' call, has resonated well with a number of contributors to this book.

Young people particularly want action on the climate. Evan Burgess, Welsh Youth Parliament member for Aberconwy, sees the Act as critical to Wales becoming a world leader on a radical climate agenda and asks for it to be made 'easy for Welsh citizens to make good decisions for the climate', continuing, 'This means taking radical action to invest in renewable energy and sustainable transport infrastructure, such as electric rail and cars. To discourage polluting industries and boost and protect the environment through expanding and protecting green areas.'

Dan Tram, One Young World delegate (Wales) calls for a law that 'charges for waste, both domestically and commercially, to challenge us all to consider the actual "need", becoming far more economical and considering reuse rather than refuse' – which fits well with a zero-waste Wales agenda.

Emily-Rose Jenkins, also an One Young World delegate (Wales), calls for new legislation to 'consider infrastructure as a multi-disciplinary "building for the future" function'. Kian Agar, Welsh Youth Parliament member for Aberavon, is clear that 'each of the goals play a vital part in the development of a new Wales and . . . if addressed properly, may solve all social and environmental issues that we face today and most definitely will in the future, directly affecting myself, my generation and many generations to come'.

Mishan Wickremasinghe, president of the Students' Union at the University of South Wales, and Vashti Miller, Graduate Health Communications Consultant at MHP Communications, both celebrate the holistic nature of the Act as the permission to think differently about health in a way which can lead to new ways of thinking and working – in Mish's case to take a new approach to mental health through social prescribing; in Vashti's, using a holistic preventive approach to policy development: 'In the simplest sense, by ensuring the collaboration between budgets, public bodies and organisations, preventative health care can be introduced.'

What is notable from all these contributions is how innovative and responsible these voices are. The young voices, in particular, have no difficulty in cross-cutting thinking. The next iteration of 'The Wales We Want' will be starting this year – I can't wait to see what people across Wales want to do, now that they have an act to help them achieve it.

'My research proves that real projects, visible change and new technology turn the tide towards hope. Not speeches, nor manifestos or compelling rhetoric – but tangible action within a community can spark a light of belief in the future and eagerness to help get us there. What Wales has proven is that village by village, town by town and within every community, actually rolling up the sleeves and making bold sustainability policy a reality does more than affect nature, it can bring hope and energy to people who need it.'

Solitaire Townsend, co-founder, Futerra, author of *The Happy Hero*

'The Act lacks teeth. People only really change their bad old ways if they have to. My wish then is that further legislation adopts the principle of contraction and convergence: that by law, every year, the ecological footprint of the country must be reduced – until after, say, 20 years, it is down to one planet.'

David Thorpe, author of *The One Planet Life* and *'One Planet' Cities*

'We need strong leadership to develop a bold vision and to deliver it. We need to take risks and be honest about our performance; learning lessons and sharing best practice.'

Nick Miller, director, Miller Research (U.K.)

CHAPTER 4

Truth-telling

Keeping the Pressure
on the Act and Its Ambition

Truth telling: a system cannot function well if its information
streams are corrupted by lies . . .
Not: unrelieved pessimism
Nor: sappy optimism
But: the resolve to tell the truth about both the successes
and failures of the present and the potentials and
obstacles in the future
And above all: the courage to admit and bear the pain of
the present, while keeping a steady eye on a vision of a
better future.

DONELLA MEADOWS

I'm writing this book in my tiny attic office, directly above the kitchen range that is fed throughout the winter by wood from our woodland, so rain or shine, day or night, I'm warm as toast. Above me is a large Velux window through which I experience the weather – mostly distantly due to our levels of insulation, but always immediately, separated from the full force of the elements by only a couple of centimetres of double glazing. And what a show the weather has put on while I've been writing, with rain, snow, hail, sunshine and showers in quick succession. The only regular sounds that have disturbed my concentration are the daily thuds and thumps of heavy birds coming in to land on our roof: mostly in the crow family – ravens, magpies, rooks, jackdaws – all glossy and well fed and ominously spread out along the telephone wire cawing in unison like foretellers of doom. Interestingly, the collective noun for crows is a 'murder', which seems appropriate for the loss of the smaller species we used to see.

We now live in a world of superlatives. Gone are the securities of seasons as I've known them throughout my life. In the six months in which this book has been written, I have lived through the hottest month in the hottest decade since records began in 1880, and I've witnessed the worst flooding in the U.K. since 2007; it has affected thousands of homes and cost hundreds of millions of pounds.

In my own garden, where I've fed birds for 10 years, I've seen a gradual but dramatic change to garden and farmland birds – fewer swallows nesting under our eaves, the loss of the cuckoo which used to herald spring, and generally less variety at the bird table, with the small birds now outnumbered by rooks, pigeons, crows, jackdaws and magpies. The latest U.K. *State of Nature* report points out that that more than a quarter of our mammals are facing extinction, with 41 per cent of species studied having experienced decline since 1970. One of those threatened species is the woodcock, a nocturnal, cryptic, elusive wading bird, adapted for a life in woodland and fields with short stumpy legs, camouflage feathers for the woodland floor and a long straight beak. By gardening organically and creating spaces for worms and insects, we've ensured this shy woodland bird is still nesting in our woodland every year. This is our wake-up call to action to maintain and encourage new habitats. We must heed it.

Truth-telling: are we thinking differently now?

As a child, watching bushfires in Africa, I was in awe of their power to consume, watching flames jump considerable distances, first caressing, then ravaging everything in their path. Watching a fire at night light up the sky, amplified by the keening sounds of terrified animals fleeing its hungry flames, is a vision of hell that we should do all in our power to avoid.

Greta Thunberg warned us that 'our house is on fire'. The Australian Prime Minister Scott Morrison was rightly faced with angry scrutiny in late 2019 for his unquestioning support for the coal industry when the fire chiefs battling the unprecedented wildfires that consumed hundreds of houses in New South Wales and Queensland told him in no uncertain terms that climate change was the reason that Australia is now in 'a new age of unprecedented bushfire danger'.

> *The Act is . . . remarkable in terms of its breadth, its coverage and ambition. There's nothing quite like it anywhere else in the world at this point.*
>
> JONATHAN BOSTON, Professor of Public Policy,
> Wellington School of Business and Government,
> Victoria University of Wellington, New Zealand

There is a particularly desperate sadness in the loss of lives of the brave firefighters trying to hold back the very power that we as humans have unleashed. Perhaps this is finally the moment when public opinion will help curtail the future of fossil fuels.

In my view the Well-being of Future Generations (Wales) Act is a beacon of hope in a time of despair. There are opportunities for new networks to be created, for new actions to come forth and new truths to be formed. What I will be exploring in this chapter and the next are, as Donella Meadows says, 'the successes and failures of the present and the potentials and obstacles in the future'.

This chapter moves the story on from the action to reaction, from creation to reflection – the truth-telling. I look at how the Act is delivering on the collective vision laid out in 'One Wales, One Planet' of a sustainable Wales (to find this vision in full, please see appendix 1 – I think it's incredibly inspiring and hopeful, and I think you will find it well worth the read). I explore what the collective will that created the Act wants to achieve in the immediate future and give early exemplar case studies from Wales that demonstrate the new ways of thinking and working.

In the spirit of truth-telling, I also explore key questions that others have posed to me and I have then posed to others. This is an area fraught with difficulty! Each of us might have an idea of what good looks like, but we may not share the same vision. When I'm asked whether I think the Act is living up to its promise or whether more scale and more pace are needed, the answer is not simple. There is a common view (that I share) that we need greater scale and pace, but that doesn't yet mean that the Act can't live up to its promise.

Perhaps the question I should have asked is whether the Act can deliver the fundamental change I proposed in the first place – and that will take time to answer. The key question that commentators and practitioners come back to, time and time again, is whether the 'permission to think differently' is the right focus for the legislation. This is a really important question to explore at the heart of the Welsh approach – the tension between those who want more enforcement or compliance mechanisms in the Act itself and those who want the Act to encourage new kinds of sustainable behavior and to outlaw unacceptable behavior, but to have compliance mechanisms in companion legislation, rather than in the Well-being Act. The Act does allow for judicial review, and the Future Generations Commissioner has substantial powers to name and shame, but that leads straight to another key question – does the Commissioner have enough powers? Certainly, the current Commissioner thinks there are some changes that would be beneficial to carrying out her role; these will be explored during the parliamentary procedures currently under way for a Well-being of Future Generations (U.K.) Act, building on the Welsh Act.

Inspiration for the future?

The very creation of the Act releases it to the people – the people in Wales who have now been given their government's permission to have wild ideas about what different paths their country, their community and their individual households could follow.

Truth-telling

The fundamental questions must be whether, in 10 years' time, Wales will be governed differently because of the Act, and whether the Act will inspire new and different actions in Welsh communities.

Almost as soon as the Act became law, I was asked to comment on its 'success'. This remains difficult. After all, the Welsh Government has been on an explicit journey over some 20 years to try to embed sustainable development into its decision making, and one could reasonably argue that it has failed to do so – at least at the level of system change. However, I'm still in awe of the fact that it is that same government that was prepared to put into law a framework that requires it and all of its agencies to explicitly commit itself to look after the interests of future generations – and to be called to account for its actions by an external commissioner. This is a real acknowledgement that its values in support of acting sustainably remain intact, not least under my old friend Mark Drakeford, the current First Minister of Wales. To hear him and Shan Morgan, the Permanent Secretary (the top civil servant), say categorically at an event held to celebrate 20 years of devolution in 2019 that the Well-being of Future Generations (Wales) Act is now really driving the Welsh policy agenda in government and public services was wonderful.

In Shan's words:

> There are unprecedented challenges facing governments across the world and public servants play an integral role in finding innovative solutions and supporting change. Wales' twenty-year devolution journey has put at its heart sustainable development and is intertwined with the development of the Welsh Civil Service. As Permanent Secretary, I take our organisational commitment to the sustainable ways of working under the Well-being of Future Generations Act extremely seriously. I have used the Act to underpin my Future Proofing initiative which is ensuring a confident, skilled and sustainable civil service in Wales now and for the future. Collaboration is at the heart of this and the Act provides a common purpose and framework for one Welsh public service working together to achieve the well-being goals and a sustainable Wales.

#futuregen

The Act provides constructive challenge to the ways we do things, and I have seen how it enables better debate, discussion and decisions within Welsh Government; with partners; and between government and citizens on the 'wicked' issues communities face. For me, this is about how countries can govern better for the future, whilst delivering now for their citizens. It is about the power of new ideas with the permission to think differently and the Act provides the firm foundations to this.

Systems change is a messy and unpredictable business. Government is only one agency in the process and by its very nature operates 'business as usual' unless it is required to change – or requires itself to change, as the Act has done in Wales. A government creating the legal environment for its own change is almost unprecedented. However, there are clear cultural shifts that the Act is facilitating inside and outside government.

It is interesting to see other countries turning to the Act as a source of inspiration for responding to the global challenges we all face. Does focusing on future generations – a concept that in principle we all support irrespective of political party or individual belief systems – enable us to have more reasoned debates about global challenges such as climate change? Could the Welsh experiment lead to other countries making their own similar but different laws? Could we see the creation of a wide and influential network of Future Generations Commissioners sharing good practice across the world?

What I can say, on the back of the research I've done for this book, is that there is a strong appetite for the Act among the people of Wales and that green shoots are popping up in the most unexpected places. Everywhere, people are starting to use the Act when they want to challenge their perception of unsustainable behaviour. Each challenge is building precedents for the future.

What is so clever about the way the Well-being of Future Generations (Wales) Act was finally crafted, through its civil society and political inputs, is that it created a law requiring the government not just to make sustainability its central organising principle, but also to set up a legislative framework for a positive vision for a responsible and sustainable Wales in harmony with nature (as outlined in 'One Wales, One Planet'). At the most basic level, this will make it much harder to repeal in the future, but in addition to this, it has also released a collective imagination that can envision a different kind of future. The Public Services Boards (the local groupings of public services organisations) charged by the Act to work together to achieve sustainable outcomes are reporting more imaginative ideas coming forward, particularly in line with low carbon prosperity and tackling climate change. The Act envisages communities which are safer, healthier, more equal, more environmentally responsible and happier. This appears to be touching a chord at the local level – and town and community councils are keen to expand their role in its delivery.

The Act in practice: early signs of take-up

There is an excitement about the opportunity to think differently, to Act differently. What used to be subversive talk, particularly from young professionals about the public sector becoming 'one service' to integrate needs and delivery holistically (as Rhodri Morgan always wanted), we now see as an explicit commitment from the Permanent Secretary, because of the Act.

There are new disruptive conversations at the local level about what communities want to do for themselves and how that can be facilitated through the act's permission, rather than seeing the state as the answer. Calls for more explicit commitments to tackle existential challenges, such as climate change and biodiversity loss in an integrated way, are starting to be heard. There are conversations about food security and regenerative agriculture that I've never heard before. In a country that produces so little of its own fruit and vegetable needs and relies so heavily on chemicals, this is a real breakaway from business as usual.

It is hard to capture the shifts in thinking until the Act has had a longer time in which to embed, but I do think the people of Wales are starting to understand its opportunities. A second 'The Wales We Want' engagement is planned before the next Assembly election in 2021 to help inform the politicians and public services. I will feel the Act is a success when the general public of all ages use it successfully to argue against unsustainable propositions.

Truth-telling: my review of the Act so far

Generally, people feel it is too early in the new Act's life for a review. After all, the Act was only introduced in 2016; in the first two years, public bodies had to undertake baseline assessments and develop plans, and those plans are only into their second year now. The first election that will test its political influence is not until May 2021. However, with a 20-year background in trying (and mostly failing) to deliver a comprehensive organisational approach, I have drawn together my own early thoughts through conversations with the key actors.

The best inspiration is truth.

PROFESSOR MEDWIN HUGHES,
Vice Chancellor, University of Wales

Achieving the well-being objectives

Early evidence from the Welsh Government suggests that in its view, it is the collective endeavour of the government, as a public body, that must achieve the well-being objectives. Commissioner Sophie Howe's interpretation is that each individual decision by a public body must seek to achieve the well-being objectives set. To argue that decisions can relate to one department or to one domain of well-being is, she argues, to undermine the spirit of the legislation. I agree with her. The Welsh Government and the Welsh public services should be aiming to live up to the spirit of the legislation. They need to be pushing the boundaries of their behaviour on the art of the possible, not restricting compliance to a minimalist approach.

Truth-telling

The four dimensions/domains of well-being

The addition of 'culture' to the usual three domains (environment, society and economy) is an important contribution that I would recommend to any country deciding to go down this route and one that we first added into 'One Wales, One Planet'. This is because I believed then and now that changing 'culture' (including history, heritage, identity, language *and* organisational culture) is the most powerful tool to create the marriage between evidence and empathy needed to enable the delivery of a future generations' framework. Unless the culture and values of an organisation change – its hearts and minds, as the Act encourages – there will be rhetoric rather than action. We have had too much rhetoric and not enough action! I hope that reframing the debate in this positive, future-oriented way will draw more people to engage at local and national level in thinking and acting more sustainably. It is critically important in particular that the Act is not seen to be in the 'culture' of any one political party but is a tool for the people of Wales to hold their government and public services to account by calling for a change to the current consumerist, wasteful, throw-away society.

Another significant intervention by the Commissioner has been her expectation that one domain *cannot* override the others – between, for example, the economic domain of well-being (the usual government measure) and the environmental, cultural and social domains. The balancing in this revolutionary act means weighting each element as equally as possible and not allowing one to tip the scales, using the best available or most reliable evidence to inform decision making, and a careful and rigorous analysis of the policy options (including their respective costs and benefits) and their distributional impacts, now and in the future.

Five ways of working

The fact that the Act requires the greater consideration of issues for the long term by public bodies, in addition to government, is hugely important. Public bodies are not usually under the same electoral pressures as their politicians. They are run by experts and should already be taking all relevant considerations into account. The Act's framework says *how* they must make their decisions (considering all relevant factors) – but *what* decision they take is up to them. The Act does not in any way cut across the expertise of organisations, or of democracy. In fact, it has been warmly welcomed for its repurposing of the very factors that many people went into public service careers to take forward – the preventive agenda and working with others to tackle the causes of the problem, rather than a reactive agenda which is problem-focused.

The seven well-being goals

What excited me about the creation of these goals is that they make it clear that public bodies can no longer work in siloed areas but are required to work collaboratively to achieve all the goals, not just one or two.

What is worthy of note, as I described in chapter 3 – and may well be unique – is that 'a prosperous Wales' is now redefined in law as low carbon, delivering within environmental limits and capable of generating decent work. This is a massive change from the unicorn of unrestricted growth and is a brave definition which I hope will have worldwide resonance, particularly among those countries declaring climate emergencies.

However, there are still major concerns, particularly among environmental groups, that the definition of 'a resilient Wales' ('a nation which maintains and enhances a biodiverse natural environment with healthy functioning ecosystems that support social, economic and ecological resilience and the capacity to adapt to change [for example climate change]') has had the weakest implementation to date because there are no direct government objectives relating to its delivery. The key word is 'enhances'. We have seen so much biodiversity loss that public policy in all areas needs to actively address this. The resilient Wales goal may still be insufficiently understood among policy makers and public services, but this will be an area that the Commissioner will need to watch closely. I take some heart from the fact that the current First Minister, Mark Drakeford, has explicitly recognised the biodiversity crisis and has prioritised the creation of institutional structures to enable this priority's delivery. He also has specifically referenced ecosystem services and benefits in supporting social and economic resilience.

The role of the Auditor General for Wales

Probably the most important contributor (apart from the Future Generations Commissioner) to the application of continuous pressure towards more sustainable performance in Wales is the Auditor General (AGW), who has a centrally important role in how the Act is taken forward in Wales. This duty is unique among auditors. Under the Act the AGW must assess the extent to which public bodies have acted in accordance with the sustainable development principle when setting their well-being objectives and in taking steps to meet those objectives. The AGW must examine each public body at least once in a five year period and present a report on the examinations to the National Assembly for Wales before each Assembly election. This requires auditors to examine *how* organisations are working to prevent problems from occurring in the first place, taking auditors into the unfamiliar territory of culture and behaviour – including whether bodies are considering the wider impact they can have on social, economic, environmental and cultural well-being and how public bodies work with one another and the communities they serve to achieve this.

Making the AGW the lead was very important to me in my original proposals, as I wanted the body that is in charge of reporting on public sector performance to be in charge of leading the change in focus of the public sector. The work of public sector auditors is still generally dominated by financial auditing, so requiring the budgets of the government and the public sector to contribute to the seven goals and other performance measures will be the next logical step for all public bodies. The next step for the Wales Audit Office is to adopt sustainable development as its central organising principle.

When AGW Adrian Crompton asked how the Audit Office itself should change in response to the Act: 'Public bodies were emphatic that the examinations needed to avoid a focus on compliance and instead focus on culture and behaviours. They also felt the auditors needed to get out into their organisations. So that's what I and my auditors did.'

Truth-telling: sustainable development in practice

Even at this early stage, we can see how the Act is inspiring different behaviours through real living changes in the public, private and community sectors.

How is the Act enhancing civil society influence?

Town centre regeneration: Usk is an affluent, historic town close to the English border. It faces profound challenges: responding to the decline of the traditional high street, ever-increasing levels of traffic, increased flood risk and a profound question of how the wider agricultural landscape should be managed. The local authorities used the Act to initiate a community-driven plan. Global urban design experts Arup were invited to help shape and direct the plan. The Act was instrumental in creating the consensus to frame a new vision of a resilient town by adopting a 'cathedral thinking' approach; by using the five ways of working to focus minds on creating alternative actions such as reclaiming streets and spaces for walking and cycling, rather than reacting to complaints about traffic. A new strategy to underpin local businesses aims to develop circular economies, linking businesses with local producers. The plan challenges the local authority to improve biodiversity, deliver sustainable tourism and provide low-carbon energy including a community-owned solar farm.

Supporting local public space: Wrexham Council supported the creation of Tŷ Pawb – a covered market owned by the council, in need of refurbishment and losing trade. Using the Act and its focus on long-term thinking and collaborative working, the council has supported the re-creation of the building as an arts and cultural centre, and, through involving local people and businesses, they have created a space which is a street-food market, marketplace, gallery, arts and crafts school, cinema and more – providing multiple benefits for the town centre local economy and people.

How is the Act creating new opportunities to live and learn differently?

One Planet Developments (OPDs): I introduced OPDs in 2010 as a planning opportunity unique to Wales where individuals could buy rural or edge-of-settlement land at agricultural prices if they are prepared to live zero-carbon lives, work the land for half national income, improve biodiversity and be subject to tight monitoring for five years. The purpose of the policy was to encourage particularly young people onto the land at affordable prices and develop a whole new generation of pioneers for sustainable living.

Many more applications have been granted since the Act, as a good OPDs planning application encompasses all the goals and ways of working. There are over 45 such developments in Wales now, both individual and community holdings, including the first planned eco-village in the U.K., and the number is growing every year. There is substantial interest in this policy in other countries and huge variation in the activities it encompasses from traditional smallholding to mushroom farming, fruit farming, willow farming (for sculpture and biomass), agroforestry, livestock, woodland management. Campaigners are now looking for more urban opportunities to open up the policy to a much wider group of potential applicants.

In '**Rethinking Business for a Changing World**', the new Carmarthen Business School at my own university, the University of Wales Trinity Saint David, started its mission to change the nature of business as a discipline in higher education when the Act was passed. They began with a clean sheet of paper to design a series of undergraduate and postgraduate programmes underpinned by sustainable and ethical and responsible thinking. Within each module students study an aspect of business through a sustainability lens which draws from the Sustainable Development Goals and the Well-Being of Future Generations (Wales) Act 2015. The business school strives to ensure that our graduates are equipped with the understanding, empathy and creativity to improve the economic, social, environmental and cultural well-being of both Wales and other nations. New course options include an online postgraduate certificate in One Planet Governance and an MBA in sustainable leadership. The business school won the U.K.'s top Green Gown Award in the Tomorrows' Employees category in 2018.

An unexpected outcome has been the level of interest that these new programmes have generated amongst local and regional business, including a new economic partnership with the local council. We have been approached by many organisations that want to work with us and our students through internships and project work.

Universities have a key role to play, says Professor Medwin Hughes, Vice Chancellor at University of Wales: 'The potential of the Well-being of Future Generations Act offers us as educationalists the opportunity of establishing a "futures orientated" pedagogy which places "placemaking" and "stewardship" at the core of our interpretation of sustainable well-being. Time is not on our side. The need for fostering a new generation of leaders who appreciate the value of a "disruptive socio-environmental capital" which can be used to further a common good should be at the forefront of our educational system.'

How is the Act arresting high-carbon activity?

M4 Relief Road: Since 1991 business organisations in Wales have sought to build a new six-lane motorway as a gateway into southeast Wales from England in a bid to tackle the congestion faced by motorists. Three times the decision was deferred by Welsh economy ministers on the grounds of cost (around £1.4 billion) and adverse effects on the environment. Following a recent formal planning enquiry which recommended support, the First Minister refused to give his consent, saying the project would have an adverse impact on wildlife, sites of special scientific interest and historic landscapes and that in his judgement the environmental concerns outweigh the road's advantages, not least since the capital cost was eye-wateringly high. Subsequently, he specifically referenced the Act and the government's declaration of a climate emergency as reasons underpinning his decision. Environmentalists – including me – were delighted!

How is the Act changing how public services are delivered?

Public sector 'Living Wage' employers: The Living Wage is an independent movement of businesses, organisations and people who believe a fair day's work deserves a fair day's pay. Organisations that pay the Living Wage have reported significant improvements in quality of work, reductions in staff absence and turnover, and a stronger corporate reputation. Paying the Living Wage to employees is vital, both in developing a sustainable economy in Wales and in telling organisations in the poorest country in the U.K. to deliver on the Act's mission to make Wales a fairer, more sustainable nation. The Welsh Government has asked all public organisations in Wales to become Living Wage employers. My own university voluntarily supported this approach; it was recently accredited, and all Welsh universities are likely to be accredited within the year.

Public sector collaborative food procurement: The Welsh Government created a Foundational Economy Challenge Fund in 2019 to introduce innovative ways of working in the spirit of the Act to support the basic goods and services on which every citizen relies and which keep us safe, sound and civilised – care and health services, food, housing, energy, construction, tourism and retailers on the high street.

The Public Services Board in Carmarthenshire has successfully applied to the Challenge Fund to use the Well-being of Future Generations (Wales) Act to change the role of public sector food procurement to support improved access to healthy, local food and create guaranteed markets for food producers. It aims over the next year to create a double dividend: a *health dividend* by promoting good food for all (especially in schools, where the citizens of tomorrow are acquiring their skills, habits and tastes today), and an *economic dividend* by securing more contracts for micro-, small- and medium-sized businesses that are locally or regionally based, with a real focus on supplier development. The board hopes that this pilot will lead to the majority of food in hospitals and schools across Wales being sourced locally within five years. The project aims to establish a new way of working, not just for the food sector but potentially across all other public sector procured goods and services in the region and, if successful, across Wales. It is being watched with interest by the rest of the U.K.

This exciting Welsh case study and others feature in *Field Guide for the Future*, the good-practice guide from the RSA's 2019 Food, Farming and Countryside Commission – the most downloaded document in the history of the RSA, directed by Sue Pritchard, a Welsh organic farmer.

How is the Act making a difference to climate change?

Transport for Wales and Metro committed to 100 per cent renewable electricity for all stations and the electrification of tracks on the lines that serve the South Wales valleys, with half of this energy being produced in Wales.

South Wales Fire and Rescue Service, and Caerphilly and Conwy Councils have rolled out solar panelling on their own buildings and community buildings, such as schools.

Monmouthshire County Council have developed a solar farm on council-owned land in Crickhowell that has the capacity to generate enough electricity to power around 1,400 homes. It will also save over 2,000 tonnes of CO_2 per year by generating clean, renewable energy. Riversimple, a small, innovative hydrogen car manufacturer based in Wales, are preparing to run a 12-month trial of 20 hydrogen fuel cell cars in Monmouthshire.

Councils have been asked to commit to becoming carbon-neutral by 2030 with major investment in the advancement of marine energy, including the pioneering 320-megawatt Swansea Bay Tidal Lagoon potentially powering a floating island of up to 1,000 homes.

How is the Act making a difference in housing?

Homes as power stations: Homes have been retro-fitted with state-of-the-art energy-efficiency technology and new, highly energy-efficient homes have been constructed over a five-year period. As well as helping cut carbon emissions, this project will also tackle fuel poverty and meet the need for more housing.

The City and County of Swansea have built 18 homes for social rent, designed to the very low-energy Passivhaus standards, meaning they need very little energy for heating and cooling, helping to keep fuel bills low.

Cartrefi Conwy housing association have a property and training subsidiary called Creating Enterprise which has started a modular house factory in Holyhead, which uses timber to build homes in less than two weeks. The homes are low energy, which can save residents up to 90 per cent in energy costs, and through reducing heat loss there is a minimal environmental impact.

How is the Act making a difference to transport?

The City and County of Swansea have bought 40 electric vehicles and won an award for the most electric vans in a public sector fleet. Caerphilly County Borough Council with Stagecoach, as well as Cardiff and Newport Councils, are in the process of introducing electric buses.

Cardiff Council is prioritising clean air and a shift from private car travel to walking, cycling and public transport. Initial concept designs have been prepared for four cycle superhighway routes, together with cycle infrastructure schemes and the on-street cycle hire scheme (with nextbike).

Using the Act, the Cardiff Public Services Board decided to take a holistic approach to transport and its impacts, not only on physical health but also on mental well-being. All partners agreed to prioritise a shift by staff and visitors to more sustainable modes of travel. A consultant in public health medicine now works one day a week with Cardiff Council's transport team on issues, including the city's clean air plan.

#futuregen

How is the Act making a difference in health?

For Ros Jervis, Director of Public Health, a key consideration for moving to West Wales was the Well-being of Future Generations (Wales) Act 2015 because of how crucial support is: 'Either through effective legislation or good policy, for the practical drive we need to enable asset-based, community-inspired change.'

Hywel Dda University Health Board has published their first long-term strategy (20 years). They've stated their main strength in relation to the Act has been the recognition that achieving improvements in health and well-being needs to be 'driven by emphasis on how we change culture and focus more on prevention, early intervention and community care to keep people well' which they believe 'demonstrates how we are seeking to "live and breathe" the principles of the Act in our everyday business'.

How is the Act helping to design out waste?

Reuse and refurbishment of furniture through circular economy procurement: Public Health Wales used the Act to adopt a new mindset when moving office in 2016 and sought suppliers who could reuse and remanufacture as much already owned furniture as possible. The winning tender provided a design in which 94 per cent of furniture was reused or remanufactured. The contract was delivered by a consortium of responsible suppliers, including a sustainable office design company, a local furniture manufacturer and a community interest company. This case study has led to the rules for public sector refurbishment across Wales being rewritten.

Eifion Williams, CEO of Circular Economy Wales, reports that in the year this book goes to press, Wales will launch a mutual credit system, piloted by Circular Economy Wales:

Local enterprises within the membership provide each other the goods and services they need to operate, whilst the system's Community Brokers record and oversee the continual process of balancing deficit and credit. Not having to deplete cash reserves for business-to-business transactions will liberate Wales' small and medium-sized enterprises sector, providing the economic cushion that currently only businesses in Switzerland, Sardinia and mainland Italy enjoy. In practical terms, Wales' CELYN Mutual Credit will provide the resilience and inter-dependence that my village could have done with in recent decades, to keep the doors open, helping maintain jobs and services in the face of economic storms.

How is the Act helping to enhance biodiversity?

National Forest: Specifically linked to the Act, the First Minister's personal manifesto for his election in 2018 was to create a new national forest. Ethiopia's successful planting of 350 million trees in one day in 2019 is a good model to follow! We'll have to see how many trees can be planted in Wales in 2020, although perhaps we should start by not importing trees from other countries when we don't know their provenance or what diseases they might carry.

Regenerating Our City for Well-being and Wildlife is an ambitious plan for Swansea (the second biggest city in Wales and a coastal city) to become greener and more resilient to climate change, using nature to provide space for wildlife, bring people pleasure and offer an improved experience for visitors and traders. The plan proposes new green infrastructure to provide an opportunity for nature to be brought into the heart of the city to widen its appeal to residents and visitors. This will bring benefits such as boosting biodiversity and improving climate change resilience.

National Museum Wales has been involved in several community-focused schemes (such as wildlife-friendly gardens at St Fagans National Museum of History developed by Hafal, the Wallich, and Innovate Trust). The GRAFT garden project at the National Waterfront Museum, Swansea, converted an unused space into a public garden, with horticulturally based courses for volunteers. At Big Pit, the Coity Tip Trail was developed to provide short walks around an old waste tip from the Coity Pit and to support wildlife, plants and natural habitats. Volunteers at the National Wool Museum created a natural dye garden and hold natural dyeing workshops.

Truth-telling: is the Act living up to its promise?

With the Act in place, I wanted to understand whether there are still key unanswered questions. Who better to ask than the wide range of people who have been involved in the Act's development, whether engaged in its delivery, scrutinising it from a civil society perspective or analysing its effects? There is a danger in sending an open email out in such circumstances, but such is the interest in the Act that I had pretty well a full house of responses! In a very unscientific way, I have raised those key questions here, collecting comments from others on how they would respond for a chapter entitled 'Truth-telling'. Here are my and their considered thoughts. I have tried to incorporate their views in the text.

How is the Act enabling young people's voices to be heard?

Wales has a long tradition of engaging with young people over policy development dating back to the beginning of the National Assembly. There are formal mechanisms – pupil councils in every school, youth forums convened at local authority level, student councils in colleges and universities and a succession of approaches to national participation through firstly Young Voice, then Funky Dragon and now the Welsh Youth Parliament.

There have been specific initiatives too – for example, the young Climate Change Champions and the Youth Forum for Sustainable Development. The Future Generations Commissioner Sophie Howe has set up a new Young Leaders Academy across Wales to advise and support her in her work. There are informal mechanisms which have culminated in Wales having the highest number of eco-schools in the U.K. with eco-committees and green flags under the European Foundation for Environmental Education (FEE) Scheme. All these forums are engaged with the Act either directly or through their adult support mechanisms – and all have become more influential because of the Act.

Most initiatives have historically been for young people older than 11, but since 2010 there has been a really exciting approach operating in Wales of empowering 'Children as Researchers' through a highly successful initiative called Lleisiau Bach / Little Voices that actively engages with children under 11. In the words of Helen Dale, coordinator of Lleisiau Bach / Little Voices: 'The very youngest children can, as well as should, be empowered as agents of change in decision-making referable to themselves and to the environment in which they too are citizens. The Children as Researchers methodology deployed in the Lleisiau Bach Little Voices projects (2012–2020) has been effective in enabling younger children to achieve real changes in their own localities as well as influencing wider society.'

Lleisiau Bach / Little Voices is rooted in the United Nations Convention on the Rights of the Child and is focused on empowering child researchers to contribute to policy development, particularly in areas which have a direct effect on them. What is particularly interesting in the current project, Little Voices Being Heard, is that primary-school-aged children through their research are calling for action on the key issues of the day: deforestation, habitats for wildlife, plastics in the oceans, endangered animals and the impact of fossil fuels.

In Wales they want more trees, more locally grown food, more wildlife. They want to see more electric/hydrogen cars, less plastic, fewer factories, reduced carbon emissions and more recycling and reusing. What is particularly hopeful is that they also want a fairer and more tolerant society which provides better support for those who are homeless or in poverty; is less selfish, kinder, more accepting of others; and most importantly listens to the views of children and young people. They are now engaging directly with public services in their local areas to argue their case, and of course the Act is very much on their side with this agenda. It will be interesting to see if the next iteration of their work, Little Voices Making a Difference, is able to use the Act to drive responses from the public bodies more in line with the young people's research, particularly when it was strongly echoed through secondary school pupils in 'The Wales We Want' and in colleges and universities through their declaration of climate emergencies.

Is the Act living up to its promise
or are more scale and pace needed?

I think that the answer depends in part on how you regard the promise that the Act holds.

At its core the Act aims to reshape the way in which we view Wales, creating a just and sustainable society functioning within ecological limits. This is extraordinarily ambitious – it requires nothing less than a paradigm shift in our world view, and while it may be a single piece of legislation that places this firmly on the agenda, it is the catalyst for change rather than the end result.

Are more scale and pace needed? The answer is unequivocal: yes. Generally, activists and commentators are impatient – they feel those in power have dragged their heels long enough; the obligation has been in place in some form for two decades, and action is needed on all fronts. There is also a feeling that more bottom-up, community-led approaches need greater support. However, there have been some welcome and significant voluntary shifts by organisations not required to deliver the Act. Some of the utilities, social housing providers and businesses are embedding the Act and reporting on it, and the Living Wage campaign in particular has been a significant success.

Is the focus on 'permission to think differently' right,
or are more compliance structures needed?

This is a tricky one. There are those who feel strongly that the only way to achieve scale and pace is to have explicit compliance mechanisms in the Act (including more powers for the Commissioner) to outlaw bad (unsustainable) behaviour. The success of my recycling legislation, which took Wales' municipal recycling to the best in the world in the second quarter of 2019, is often quoted back to me on the basis that this achievement could only have happened through enforcement. But it is worth remembering here that the recycling legislation was very specific and targeted, whereas the Act is a broad framework for thinking and behaving differently and contains many mechanisms within it – the Future Generations Commissioner, the

Auditor General for Wales, the national indicators, the milestones, the Future Trends Report, the Future Generations Report – all of which, over time, will drive the duty to deliver on the goals in policy and decision making.

If the goal is to change the culture of government and governance in perpetuity (as I believe it is), then perhaps the way through this conundrum is the creation of companion acts to enforce and compel on specific measures, particularly in relation to statutory performance measures – which is the approach I took with the recycling legislation. This places legal enforcement, if required, on a firmer footing and is already in place in terms of the Environment Act – a more traditional piece of compliance legislation working under the framework of the Well-being of Future Generations Act.

Changing the paradigm needs a suite of coordinated actions if it is to happen. Two key areas are to share best practice and reward good behaviour. The Act is the framework to exemplify what 'good' looks like; the government now needs to institute financial reward structures across its full range of responsibilities, but it must also be prepared to put in place compliance-led approaches in specific areas to deliver a more robust approach. For example, to reduce greenhouse gas emissions fast, we urgently need *far* stricter regulatory interventions.

One of the most famous quotes about democracy is from Abraham Lincoln: 'No man is good enough to govern another man without that other's consent.' I think this point is crucial. The framework I wanted to introduce in Wales in the Act is one to help people of all political persuasions make good decisions. It is not – and cannot be – anti-democratic. It provides the *how* (the framework for achieving outcomes), but the *what* (which priorities and which actions) is up to the political parties. They are constrained only to take sustainable decisions. For example, if they do want to create a new highway, they will have to think carefully about the route (avoiding designated Natura 2000 sites) and materials (using alternatives to cement, for example), which means they can create the outcome more sustainably. I'm concerned that if the compliance powers in the Act itself are too strong, it could be perceived as anti-democratic and an incoming government might choose to repeal it on that basis – and the legal framework for long-term decision making would be lost.

In 10 years' time will Wales be governed differently because of the Act?

Wales is already beginning to be governed differently because of the Act. The nature of civic discussion is being changed by the Act and the evolving culture change that it seeds and supports. The more prevalent the Act becomes in the public sphere, the more the government and public services will be held to account by the people of Wales.

There is a need to develop better ways to achieve learning (including from mistakes), measure change (tracking the journey) and audit budgets (ensuring fitness for purpose). The Act enables a new approach to governance: less of the way in which government traditionally operates (top-down, command and control) and more collaborative and participative – without which the desired well-being outcomes will be elusive.

The test will be when the Act threatens a government's own desires. To some extent this has already happened, with the M4 Relief Road and the current government's decision not to support it. A similar test may well come from the Welsh Government's ownership and management of Cardiff Airport – the same government that was the first in the U.K. to declare a climate emergency. These decisions are part of the complexity of government and require appropriately complex considerations – and they may also present new opportunities. Could Cardiff Airport, a government airport, lead on the development of alternative aviation fuel sources arising out of byproducts from the steel industry? If others follow Wales' example in legislating for future generations, there will be more opportunities for the collaborative airing of such issues and learning how to tackle such problems in the future.

The fundamental test of the Act must be whether it changes Wales' footprint on this planet – which is where the 'One Wales, One Planet' approach started. Tracking Wales' footprint annually can be a proxy indicator for the direction of travel to a more sustainable nation. But this must be a collective journey with the people of Wales, that takes the opportunity to improve the quality of their lives on the way. Less developed (poorer) countries have smaller footprints, and that is not the desired outcome – but making Wales safer, healthier, kinder, more tolerant, more equal, more prosperous, all within environmental limits, is. The opportunity is ours to take and we should take it with gusto, holding our heads high in delivering on our commitment to future generations. This should be a fundamental source of national pride and ambition, not a wrangle between bodies about how little action they can get away with!

What is the role of the National Assembly for Wales, now that the new duty only falls on Welsh ministers?

When the duty to 'promote' sustainable development was first introduced in 1998, it was a duty on the whole of the new National Assembly for Wales, the members and the executive. Following the separation of powers in 2006, the duty fell to the government, but explicitly not to the National Assembly for Wales. Nevertheless, the Assembly is a critical institution in ensuring that the Act is taken seriously by policy makers and delivers results. When reports are tabled in the National Assembly, as required under the Act, it is then up to the National Assembly and its various committees to scrutinise these reports and make recommendations to the government, including critiquing the quality of the government's performance in exercising its stewardship responsibilities in protecting long-term interests.

Early evidence indicates that Assembly Members have been asking more questions of ministers in relation to the Act and its implementation, including the work of the Commissioner. Assembly committees too have been drawing on the Act; for instance, some committees have made recommendations in their reports to incorporate the well-being objectives more fully in the government's budget processes. The government has accepted those recommendations which have also been called for by civil society.

#futuregen

How do we ensure momentum is carried across all political parties and changes in administration?

I think there are three elements to this. First, it must be about managing the daily business of government through the civil service. We have a saying in the U.K. that 'whoever you vote for, the government still gets in'. This means that the civil service – the government officials – are still there writing the government papers, whoever has been elected politically. Culture change in the civil service is therefore absolutely critical. The Act is now starting to become the mechanism that has been called for in every effectiveness review, but this requires leadership from the very top – the Permanent Secretary and her team of director generals – to explicitly lead and require delivery. The commitment of the current Permanent Secretary is heartening, and both the Future Generations Commissioner and the Auditor General for Wales have key roles in helping government on its journey.

Politically, the more left-of-centre parties – sometimes described as the 'progressive' parties – which have supported the legislation from the outset, are increasingly using it both to promote actions and to call actions to account. The most enthusiastic parties have been Welsh Labour (the government party) and Plaid Cymru (the main opposition party) with support from the Liberal Democrats as well.

One proposition that has come forward from civil society is for the political parties to formally agree to uphold the Act as a Welsh national vision – a constitutional commitment. This has a number of potential benefits. It acknowledges that the Act arose from the first Government of Wales Act – a constitutional instrument – and a revision to the next Government of Wales Act would enable the Well-being of Future Generations Act to also apply to the National Assembly, as did the initial duty. I strongly support this. I was sorry that the separation of powers in 2006 took the duty away from the National Assembly, and I loved that the first iteration of the commitment was in the founding constitutional document for Wales. I hope that the National Assembly, which has also declared a climate emergency, does want to take the commitment forward.

Truth-telling

The first key test of the breadth of the Act's reach will be the degree to which it shapes proposals for the next Welsh general election in 2021 following the publication of the twin reports in 2020 by the Future Generations Commissioner and the Auditor General for Wales.

How does the Act meet and respond with appropriate actions to a changing climate, an increasingly elderly population, potentially dramatic changes to the local economy arising from Brexit, artificial intelligence and other geopolitical challenges? It would be hard to argue that Wales on its own can influence the big drivers (technological, economic, environmental, et cetera) that will largely affect our destiny and that of the rest of the world. A critical issue, however, is whether the Act encourages and enables Wales to adapt to change, prepare better for future negative impacts (sea level rise, for example), seize new opportunities that will contribute to a more sustainable and resilient future and thus be seen as a global future generations leader by its actions.

Is Wales too small? The question of size

My experience as a minister trying to innovate has always bumped up against those who were resistant to change, particularly those who had never supported the transfer of powers to the Welsh Government. Two killer facts would be cited: that Wales is too small to alter global outcomes, and that it lacks sufficient powers, influence and money to be effective.

I firmly believe Wales is small enough to innovate, yet big enough to matter. Wales is a microcosm of the world. Our biodiversity loss can only be remedied locally; the protection of our seas can only happen locally; our mitigation or adaptation in relation to the changing climate can only happen locally. Our support for our people can only happen locally, and we can put forward strong arguments to the U.K. Government of the day for any levers we need to deliver. Not making these changes locally would be the same abdication of government responsibility we have seen across the world. Yes, of course, we need action on international treaties; however, individual countries acting in the interests of future generations is a potent and powerful message that we care about future generations and can help pave the way for others to take similar action, building a hopeful future by developing new partnerships and expertise across the world.

The challenge in relation to the limited nature of our devolved powers is a more robust one. Welsh decision makers do not have control over many of the essential policy levers, including monetary and fiscal policy; international relations, trade and security; the level and provision of benefits to the poorest in society; and many areas of economic, social and environmental regulation. Hence the Welsh ability, for example, to alter income and wealth distribution or alleviate poverty within Wales is very modest.

I accept this challenge fully. The idea that you don't do the best you can within the resources available to improve the lives of your citizens is anathema to me. We should always be looking outward to networks of change which can help us on our journey.

The behaviour change required by the Act is less about money and more about the level and coherence of our ambition; changing our priorities, building on the character and landscape of Wales and the characteristics of its land and people. There are many economists and policy experts who argue that good, collaborative, long-term decision making, tackling the causes of problems rather than their effects, would be more effective than crisis-led policy spending.

It's also worth pointing out that just as the geology of Wales led to the first industrial revolution fuelled by coal, the geography of Wales is well placed to fuel the second with its wealth of renewable energy resources (prevailing winds, sun, abundance of water, the height of our tides) and strong communities. Perhaps we should try to use the bio-regionalism of Wales more cleverly – imagine a mosaic of communities defined by geography that meet their energy and food needs with local resources and have economies founded on social enterprises that in turn support an ecosystem of micro-businesses and small traders living within their environmental limits and enhancing biodiversity on the way. That would be a model worth developing in the spirit of the vision outlined in 'One Wales, One Planet'!

What are the wider global conditions that mean that others are turning to the Act as a source of inspiration?

Since 1992, through the United Nations, world governments have met to 'act' on the key issues of our day – whether that be climate change, biodiversity, global poverty, Millennium Development Goals or Sustainable Development Goals. There have been innumerable plans, strategies and commitments – some with legally binding frameworks such as the Kyoto Protocol; most without. In 2008 the U.K. Labour Government passed the Climate Change Act, with a statutory reduction target of 80 per cent by 2050, which in 2019 was amended to 100 per cent. The U.K. is still one of a very few countries in the world to enshrine net-zero into law, although now the pressure is to achieve more, earlier, with a focus on 2030 rather than 2050.

The Climate Change Act was passed in readiness for the 2009 Conference of Parties (COP 15) meeting in Copenhagen, which at its outset looked likely to come to a global agreement on an action plan. It did not. The shock realisation of that climate summit was that resistance to action was greater than anticipated; some would argue it was the effective death of ambitious multilateralism. Having attended the conference, I still remember the depressing experience of being in a room for days where people were arguing furiously over a target of keeping temperature rise to 1.5 or 2°C without agreeing a delivery mechanism. It was one of those moments that meant when I came back (by train), I was determined to deliver action at the Welsh level.

Since then governments have not been prepared to act collaboratively and decisively at the international level, while the ever-more-pressing questions posed at domestic levels as we reach and exceed planetary boundaries go on. What is becoming more prevalent is a growing concern and anxiety about the ecological crises and other problems that are afflicting the planet, particularly for young people. In 1992 I used to believe that governments didn't know about the effect of their policies, but that is not true now. What they have done, almost without exception, is legislate for the current generation and somewhat cynically pass the responsibility down the line to future generations – in the U.K. think of the Private Finance Initiative (PFI) or nuclear waste, for example.

In 1992 Earth Overshoot Day (the day in the year when humanity's resource consumption exceeds the Earth's capacity to regenerate those resources that year) was mid-October, so we were already overusing the Earth's capacity by two and a half months then.

In 2019 Earth Overshoot Day was 29 July. In twenty-seven years we have lost a further two and a half months. In broad terms that's nearly a month being notionally lost in each decade since 1992. I know it's only a tool, but it warns us that carrying on with business as usual, not looking after the interests of future generations, means within seventy years there could be no replenishment – and some of the younger readers of this book will still be alive. But luckily, even here there is hope. There was the one year when the trajectory was stemmed. One year when there was no increase. It was, of course, 2008. In a very narrow sense, the financial crash was good for our longer-term future. Tackling our consumerism and the unicorn of infinite growth is absolutely key for us and future generations.

In the widespread global quest for ways to ensure greater sustainability, the Welsh model I believe has much to commend it, not least for its redefinition of prosperity as 'innovative, productive and low carbon, acting on climate change and providing employment opportunities allowing people to take advantage of the wealth generated through securing decent work'.

What is the next step in transformational results?
Translating the Welsh Act into a U.K. act . . .

Meeting John Bird for the first time is like meeting a force of nature. Ennobled in 2015, Lord John Bird is now a crossbench peer in the House of Lords (not aligned to any political party), the appointed (not elected) revising chamber in the British parliamentary system. John has barrelled his way through life, not afraid to tell truth to power and not afraid to demand support for workable solutions to societal problems. The creation of *The Big Issue*, the world's most successful street magazine across four continents, was a revolutionary way to tackle poverty. The model he created by giving homeless people the means to take control of their own lives within a support structure by selling a fortnightly, cutting-edge, quirky, informative, accessible magazine has spread across the world.

John's latest proposition is to propose a Future Generations Bill for the whole of the U.K., building on and complementing the Welsh law. He says, 'Wales is leading the way in the world, and I must say the very idea that one of the countries of the United Kingdom had the space, the time, the energy and the desire to change the way that they encountered the future is everything I wanted to do.'

I'm delighted that this approach is being picked up by such a no-nonsense, determined and seasoned campaigner! For the last two years, John has been building a cross-party alliance of MPs and peers to create a U.K. version of the Welsh law to embed long termism, prevention and the interests of future generations at the heart of U.K. policy making, to tackle the climate crisis, poverty and health inequalities. He is mindful of the devolved governments' powers in Wales, Scotland and Northern Ireland; his proposal is for a U.K. Commissioner to have powers in relation to all the areas which are not devolved to the constituent countries, which could choose – or not – to have their own commissioners for their own responsibilities.

The U.K. bill has at its heart the same overarching principle as Wales, but proposes some distinct differences in delivery, reflecting the wider range of powers of the U.K. Government and a greater appetite for the Commissioner and for the population to hold government to account. Goals and ways of working to balance short-term and long-term needs, act preventively and forecast emerging risks will be devised through citizens' assemblies, rather than politicians. The bill will apply to larger companies in the private sector as well as the public sector. New duties will be placed on U.K. secretaries of state to publish national future trends and risks reports, taking into account the views of the United Nations in relation to the Sustainable Development Goals, the U.K. Committee on Climate Change, the United Nations Intergovernmental Panel on Climate Change, the Intergovernmental Science-Policy Platform on Biodiversity and Ecosystem Services, and, importantly, primary and secondary schoolchildren and those in further and higher education. The bill also establishes a Joint Parliamentary Committee for the Future to scrutinise legislation for its effect on future generations and hold U.K. Government ministers to account.

The U.K. bill aims to add extra 'teeth' to the Welsh Act by increasing the powers of the U.K. Commissioner, allowing them to conduct an investigation if they suspect that the public body concerned has failed to comply with its duties. There is an explicit legal right for individuals to hold named bodies to account when their duties are not being met, and individuals can request the Commissioner to initiate an investigation if they believe that a public body has failed to fulfil its duties. The U.K. bill also increases the Commissioner's remit by placing a duty on them to engage members of the public on issues affecting the long-term future of the United Kingdom, including the creation of a citizens' panel and expert panel.

John's Future Generations (U.K.) Bill is going through its parliamentary processes in 2020. A successful outcome will create even broader interest for the model. If his bill is prevented by the current U.K. Government from becoming law, it will also generate interest as a direct attack on young people's future opportunities: futures already affected by an inadequate response to climate and nature issues and the removal of the opportunities for future generations to live, work and play in the 27 other countries in the European Union. All the polling prior to our most recent U.K. election – and subsequent analysis post the election – suggests that a large majority of younger voters want action on climate change and want to stay in Europe. Tragically, it is the older generations, mostly those beyond retirement age, who have deprived the young of action on both these fronts. The very campaign for a Future Generations (U.K.) Bill will open all these issues to wider public debate.

What most excites me about this proposal is that it employs the opportunity to create laws with common desired outcomes in different countries in different ways to reflect context, culture and circumstance. This is the dividend of devolution in the U.K.! Wales' lead on introducing carrier bag charges led to implementation across the four countries of the U.K., but each with slight variations – that's what culture and learning are all about. At local authority level across the U.K., there are substantially improved recycling outcomes following the Welsh model. If a stronger law is applied at U.K. level, Wales may choose to revisit its own legislation.

There is also substantial interest in the Welsh legislation, with policy makers and academics across the world – notably in Canada, New Zealand, Portugal, Gibraltar, Australia and the United Arab Emirates – looking at the Welsh experiment with interest. More countries making such a future generations commitment could be transformative, particularly if their commissioners could work together on wider outcomes than have traditionally been discussed at conferences convened by the Intergovernmental Panel on Climate Change.

I hope that other countries would be prepared to consider legislating in a way that works for them, and that they deliver on John Rawls' fundamental proposition: 'Do unto future generations what you would have past generations do unto you.'

'Good law or policy has to be holistic in its nature – containing both yin (being) and yang (doing) in equal measure. Such a law, at root, ought to catalyse the conditions conducive for human beings to become who they truly are: life-loving, biophilic beings susceptible to wisdom.'

Giles Hutchins, author of *Future Fit* and
co-author of *Regenerative Leadership*

'Cyber security knowledge and skills are becoming vital life skills for all cyber citizens. It is now therefore an important life skill we all should integrate in our daily cyber behaviour to the extent that it becomes an unconscious action that has a result on our well-being as people.'

Nisha Rawindaran, cyber security researcher,
Cardiff Metropolitan University

'The systematic collection of gender-disaggregated data and policies guaranteeing gender balance in appointments to Cabinet, Boards, Commissions, country embassies and national delegations are essential instruments to ensure gender equality and inclusiveness as governance principles for future generations.'

Dr Betsy McGregor, author of *Women on the Ballot*;
recipient, Head of Public Service Award, Canada;
former senior research fellow, Harvard Medical School

CHAPTER 5

Learning

Living the Spirit of the Act

Learning means exploring a new path with vigour and courage, being open to other people's explorations of other paths, and being willing to switch paths if one is found that leads more directly to the goal.

DONELLA MEADOWS

One day last summer there was a wheeling spiral of six red kites above my house. Glorious birds of prey, notable for their spectacular red plumage, with their sky antics and their distinctive forked tails, they own the skies above mid-Wales. They nest in our woodland so, for us, seeing a kite is a regular occurrence, but from today's abundance it is hard to imagine that a century ago they were at risk of total extinction. The first Kite Committee, worried about their future, was formed as far back as 1903, and up to 40 years ago they were one of only three globally threatened species in the U.K., their very rarity leading to their nests in Wales being robbed of eggs. A plan was hatched to create other sites in England and Scotland, and conservation charities worked together successfully to establish self-sustaining colonies. Kites now majestically patrol the upland skies across the U.K.

The red kite has been subject to the longest continuous conservation project in the world. It is a proud symbol of conservation success and the power of humans to collaboratively intervene to tackle a known conservation problem. We have the knowledge; now let us exercise the will.

Visions for the future

To be an early adopter of a big new idea is to catapult yourself into the public eye, particularly when you are the first taking a decisive action. Others look to you for inspiration – and you may not have got it right! But if you own your commitment and vision, and do everything you can to achieve it, your experience, married to your ambition, is incredibly important in other people's learning too.

The task now is to engage the people of Wales in imagining a future of hope, a different future in which all of us can lead fulfilling creative lives, healthy in mind and body and in harmony with nature.

SIMON WRIGHT, food writer, broadcaster and restaurateur

There is a great deal of learning that we can take from Wales' journey so far. I say 'we' deliberately here, as the success of the Well-being of Future Generations Act in the end will be determined by whether it can become the Welsh people's legislation rather than a government law.

I started thinking about what tools you would need to achieve this and what my own learning has been, following the research that I have done for this book.

Reflecting back on that journey since the publication of 'Learning to Live Differently' in 2000, I think the context of the 'right' time and place for whole system change is really important. Using a disruptive moment – such as the birth of a new institution – has many merits, but it must be accompanied by an appropriate plan. The all-embracing of vision of 'Learning to Live Differently' laid the foundations for the Well-being of Future Generations Act, but without a framework for delivery, it was described as utopian. 'Starting to Live Differently' in 2004 was commended for its tighter delivery focus but was seen by some as '10 actions for a better planet' rather than the delivery of a wider vision. 'One Wales, One Planet' in 2009 reintroduced the big vision with a framework for delivery but, despite pockets of success, it also didn't manage to deliver whole system change.

At the core of system change must be both the desire to do it and a clear idea of what the culture of an organisation needs to be to deliver it. The Well-being of Future Generations Act has created the culture and environment to make that happen, but legislation on its own is not enough. There still has to be a plan!

Following my conversations with civil servants, civil society, commentators who have tracked Wales' journey and particularly young people who have contributed to the book, five learning themes that I now believe to be essential have emerged.

1. **Leadership for delivery is key.** In essence, this is a no-brainer, but it is easier to say than to do. The legal framework of the Act addresses two key problems that have been there since the 'duty to promote' was first introduced to the new National Assembly for Wales: clarity of purpose and a mechanism for delivery. Provided both are seized and become the central principle of delivery, there is no excuse for any public service in Wales to fail to deliver on the goals and ways of working. Leadership needs a focus, and the Act provides it. The people of Wales can therefore reasonably expect demonstrable changes to the organisation culture and governance of their public services because of the Act. The seven goals are a framework for challenging 'business as usual' as all organisations must maximise their contribution to all of them. They must also carry out the five ways of working to ensure better long-term decision making. This is system change in action but still needs other factors in place to deliver.

2. **The Act needs to become a 'people's act'** – a tool by which the public can hold government and public services to account on behalf of future generations, which can restore some faith in politics and which can help build the resilience and cohesion of our communities. We have seen many examples of the

priorities of people and government at odds with each other. More collaborative approaches to delivering public services – and identifying what services are important to the people of Wales in the long term – is key.

3. **The government and public services must create the right support and financial mechanisms** to enable the practical drive needed. Long-term well-being needs to be at the heart of government policies, particularly in relation to the economy. This is whole system change and requires leadership, guidance and investment. The new partnership boards of all public services created by the Act, the Public Services Boards, are a huge opportunity to reframe collaborative working at the local and regional levels, but they must be ambitious deliverers and not talking shops!

4. **Learning from others is always important.** Exemplar delivery, which has at its heart a community-based approach to a circular economy in harmony with nature, will be critical. I've highlighted in this book exciting examples of changing behaviour that are happening; this now needs to move further and faster with the use of financial and other rewards to endorse and celebrate good behaviour and disincentivise short-termism. If further legislation is needed to drive the agenda, it should be embraced.

5. **Nature has rights too!** I started this book with the premise that humans have the 'right to live in harmony with nature', which recognises nature as the foundation for ensuring a safe and secure future for future generations. As Jonathon Porritt says so eloquently, 'To be young today and suddenly aware of the now-inevitable impact of accelerating climate change on every young person's life, for the rest of their life, until the day they die, is a shocking burden they have to bear.' He also says that 'there has never been such a deeply immoral intergenerational betrayal in the history of humankind'. He is absolutely right. Somehow, we need to find a way of *really* addressing

the importance of nature, for the first time, for all our futures. Language is important here. If the goal for 'a resilient Wales' becomes the 'nature' goal, it will become a positive affirmation for action. The word 'resilience' has become slippery, like the word 'sustainable', where it can be used to describe something which is the absolute opposite of what is intended and in doing so undermine the concept. It is now my view that the single most important thing we can all do for future generations is to take all the actions needed to restore nature. That means shifting government budgets and requiring all organisations to play their part to support the recovery of nature and climate.

In this chapter I offer three visions for Wales that have been my inspiration: Morgan Parry, CEO of WWF Cymru, from whom I first really understood the need to act; an exciting new initiative, Project Skyline, a networking approach to transform the landscape of the South Wales valleys by the communities themselves; and, with a vision for government, the First Minister of Wales, Professor Mark Drakeford AM.

I also want to demonstrate my own learning, my changing sense of what is most important – and what I believe is the most fundamental challenge now: to 'permit the best of human nature, rather than the worst, to be expressed and nurtured'.

Through my childhood and early adulthood, I saw nature as a constant, a wonderful opportunity available to all of us, a place of continuity in our lives. I was so wrong. When did nature become a 'nice to have', rather than the essential underpinning of human existence?

Ecology before economy: the most important tool for our survival

For years I struggled to find a way of describing the need to reframe economic policy within environmental limits in a way that made sense. Then I met Satish Kumar, the founder of the ecologically focused Schumacher College, and the answer became blindingly clear. One of the highlights for students at Schumacher College is the evening fireside chats with Satish. When all is still, he tells a story as a prelude to a discussion. The one that stays with me most, and that I have retold probably more often than he has, is about the relation between the words 'ecology' and 'economy', which are derived from the same root – oikos. The words themselves come from three Greek words: *oikos, logos, nomos*. 'Oikos' means 'home': a place of relationships among all forms of life, sharing and participating in the evolution of the Earth community. 'Logos' means 'the knowledge of our planet home', and 'nomos' means 'the management of that home'. As knowledge should come before management, so ecology should come before economy. But at economic powerhouse universities, the study of economics has no corresponding study of ecology. Thus, universities across the globe send millions of young people into the world equipped with management skills but without knowledge of what they are going to manage.

As a university professional, I found this a particularly telling story. The clue was there in the name – and I had missed it! Ecology is the knowledge of our planet, economy the management of it. In the simplest terms, economy without ecology makes no attempt to understand the delicate balance needed between humankind and the natural world. We need an active return to first principles. How do we create an economy that enhances our ecology – and thus our survival? Currently all the evidence, particularly from the so-called developed countries, is going in the opposite direction.

Everything I've discovered since has added to that picture of woe – the global floods and the fires where nature signals loud and clear that our global behaviour has to change to bring the economy back within our ecology; at the more local level, chemicals used to grow most of our (non-organic) food for humans and animals are destroying our Welsh countryside and making it harder to tackle climate change; attempts to keep the sea out of our lives with concrete walls (and the correlated emissions). Rather than thinking long-term about arresting the consequences of climate change, even where we have annual devastating updates of species loss, we continue to destroy habitats and climate.

I'm acutely aware that if I hadn't become a minister, it may have taken me many more years to understand the bigger picture. But I also know that governments do understand the consequences of their actions, so for me the single most important thing a government can do is to act only within its environmental limits. The single most important thing we can do as individuals is to act within our own environmental limits – to take action to live as lightly on the planet as possible and, in particular, help prevent more species loss by what is traditionally called nature conservation and should be titled 'nature restoration' I've always loved the idea of nature conservation – it's somehow so very worthy! But since we have totally failed to 'conserve', I think it is time to explicitly 'restore' nature instead, which is a much more adventurous proposition. We know that there are examples across the world where if you leave nature to its own devices, biodiversity returns quickly and resilience is built once more. How can we accelerate that?

This chapter is filled to the brim with hope and love – not for an impossible or unrealistic future – but a future where human beings demonstrably exercise their right to live in harmony with nature, as first promoted by the original Earth Summit in Rio de Janeiro in 1992.

A view from the future: Wales in 2050

At the beginning of this book you will find my dedication to Morgan Parry, CEO of WWF Cymru in 2007, who was the person, more than any other, who really set me on the path that led to the creation of the Act with his publication of WWF's 'One Planet Wales' in 2007. Morgan was one of those inspirational individuals who manage to combine evidence with empathy. At the time, I was determined to be an 'evidence-based' minister, thinking evidence on its own was enough to change behaviour. I hadn't read Donella at that point or learned that culture, context and all the softer tools Donella identified are much more important in changing behaviour.

Morgan had been invited to give a major lecture at the National Eisteddfod in Wales, the largest annual celebration of a minority-language culture in Europe. He wondered whether an imaginative approach might succeed where scientific evidence had failed to communicate the urgency of the problems we face. Since 2050 had become the talismanic date by which global climate targets had to succeed and realising that his son would be 50 in 2050, he said to himself, 'It seems to me that this is one moment in our history when we need a little imagination', so, alongside the best scientific evidence, Morgan also decided to envision a successful transition to his son's 50th birthday.

Beside technological advances, he waxes lyrical about the opportunities for regenerative agriculture where a greater focus on local produce contributes to food security, actively conserving the land without the pesticides that have done so much harm to Welsh land and rivers. There is a very nature strong restoration theme too: massive tree planting to create natural flood defences, bogs and wetlands restored to hold back heavy rain from flooding valleys, with every farm now having a small reservoir for its crops in changing climate.

His prediction of Wales' successful adaptation is linked to its foresight in supporting the well-being of future generations because 'we adapted before the climate changed, and understood before anyone else what we had to do to survive . . . . We've become a more equal society, more humble, more reliant on our neighbours and the sustaining power of the land.'

He starts and ends his visionary lecture with a time-honoured golden picture of innocence: children selling honey and eggs at the farm gate – a symbolic, hopeful vision of a successful transition to a sustainable future, where there are still bees to pollinate our crops.

He closes the lecture with the following words: 'We've stopped living as if there is no tomorrow, and it feels like a new era is about to dawn.' I love that; it's a great philosophy to put into personal practice. In the lecture Morgan accepts that the small country of Wales cannot address global issues on its own, but his hopeful vision is predicated on our collective understanding in Wales, before anyone else, of what we needed to do to survive – and that we acted accordingly. His approach of envisioning what life will be like when our children are the same age as we are now makes us really consider what future we might want for our children and grandchildren and beyond – and helps us see how we can get there. The opportunity of the Well-being of Future Generations (Wales) Act is a legislative framework to deliver 'a new era'. As a philosopher of hope, Morgan, I salute you.

A vision for 2070: transforming three valleys in South Wales

My next vision for the future further eschews the old economy for a new 'economy of ecology', demonstrating a different relationship between government and local communities. Individual communities must lead their own particular journey to well-being, as well-being will have many local characteristics linked to society, economy, culture and environment, but that journey can be actively facilitated by a government setting a community free to dream, if it is willing to trust and enable them over a longer-term future.

> *We are dependent on the natural world for every breath of air we take and every mouthful of food we eat. But it's even more than that, we are also dependent on it for our sanity and sense of proportion.*
>
> SIR DAVID ATTENBOROUGH

One of the best things for me about being passionate about creating a better world for future generations is that you keep meeting wonderful people who blow you away with their ideas and commitment and who, by their very actions, encourage you and others to do more.

One such person is Chris Blake, one of the instigators of Project Skyline, an inspirational initiative to enable communities to own and manage the land that surrounds them; to imagine what that future looks like and then work to achieve it.

Skyline was born in 2019 as a community land-stewardship project to look at what would happen if the community were given back their surrounding land in perpetuity. What could happen if *all* the rights to use *all* the publicly owned land – not a few hectares for a few years, but hundreds of hectares, to the skyline, for generations – were transferred to the local towns?

What I love about this simple and visionary idea is the idea of this generation actively creating a positive future in perpetuity for future generations by giving agency to local people – in this particular case three communities which were established for specific economic reasons, in another time, in the South Wales coalfield.

When I talk about the South Wales valleys, my first visit to them when I came to live in Wales in the mid-1970s is still imprinted on my mind; only a few miles from the affluent suburb in which we lived in spacious houses and tree-lined streets, there they were, built on coal, black to the skyline in deep natural gullies, bringing the nation its fuel. My father thought it was important for us to understand the context of the place where we lived. It was a wet Sunday afternoon when we drove up the Rhondda Valley – village after village with its own mine. Close to the mines, the vegetation was bedraggled, coated lightly in grey dust, struggling for light and air. The houses, although attractively built in traditional stone, were poorly maintained with leaking windows. I was horrified that people should be living in these conditions and could see only the darkness, the dust and the uninviting black and dirty River Taff. As someone brought up in a country full of light and air, colour and wildlife, horizons that stretched to infinity, this was deeply shocking.

Fast-forward half a century and it is a different world. Nature has reclaimed the slag heaps, helped by investment in land reclamation, and the valleys are green again, alive with birdsong; people come to walk and cycle and particularly to use the world-class mountain biking routes. But still, the communities are left behind – too far from the capital, unable to take up economic opportunities along the motorway corridor linking Wales' two main cities – and you can't eat the scenery!

Over four decades substantial public and private investments have done little to improve the long-term economic prospects of the Welsh valleys. Despite capital investment in transport, schools, hospitals and an ultimately unsuccessful industrial diversification strategy, these communities are still amongst the poorest in the U.K.

The high moorland that surrounds each valley does not benefit the local economy. Where the land *is* of economic value – from forestry and wind power – it is managed by national and international corporations with little direct economic benefit to the local community.

Skyline imagines a different future – a manifestation of the Well-being of Future Generations Act at a landscape scale. A future in which the community manages the land that surrounds the town sustainably, to meet the needs of the people who live there in a way that doesn't compromise the needs of future generations; reconnecting communities to a landscape so that it can provide income, jobs, a place of social and cultural activity and a better home for nature.

Let's imagine a Skyline project in 30 years' time. The micro-hydroelectric scheme and the wind turbines sell low-cost electricity to the local community, but also light and heat the greenhouses built on the old colliery site that provide year-round vegetables. The forest school building, constructed from timber processed at the community timber yard, is part of the curriculum for all the schools and colleges and, in the evening, it is the venue for skills training in forestry, horticulture and animal welfare.

Children use the woodland as an outdoor play area, young people as somewhere to hang out, and adults can be seen making use of the different paths and trails on foot, on bike and by horse. On the western hillside, the conifers were felled a decade ago, partly for income and partly to provide timber for the new building. In its place the new broadleaf woodland now flushes pale green every spring, providing a new home for native wildlife – in another few years it will be coppiced for biomass production. A section of the land nearest the town has been leased in forest smallholdings modelled on One Planet Developments – that have attracted some new families to the valley.

Every aspect of the Well-being of Future Generations Act was explored in the process of creating each community's long-term vision for their valley. But perhaps more than anything, Skyline was built on trust: trust in a community to manage sustainably at a landscape scale, for the long term; trust that the community would be capable of balancing the potentially conflicting goals of the Act. Who better to balance the goals of prosperity, natural resilience, equality, health, and a vibrant and cohesive community with global responsibilities than the people who actually live in the place they want to transform.

To create the vision for each valley, Skyline worked with three communities in three different valleys – Caerau, Treherbert and Ynysowen – exploring the history, meaning and potential of each place and exploring the ideas of land stewardship over a period of nine months. A link to their report, full of good ideas as to how to co-create a vison and plan, is in appendix 2.

I asked Chris to reflect on the process and the outcomes:

We started by working with artist facilitators. Starting conversations to engage the heart and the imagination first. Developing trust, exploring ideas without constraint.

We took community members to Scotland to see what 25 years of Scottish community land reform had delivered. It turned an abstract idea into something real. 'If they can do that, then we can too.'

We assembled the technical experts on forestry management, successful business models, ecology and land law, but made sure that this technical expertise must be used to serve and not lead the plans and visions of the community.

We worked with as wide a cross section of the community as we could so that any future landscape change will have the widest acceptance.

We worked in close collaboration with all of the agencies – the landowner, the land manager, the local authority, starting the process of building trust.

Learning

Asking the people of Ynysowen in the Merthyr Valley, we got these dreams and reflections . . .

the skyline is for looking at
the skyline is the Taff trail
flowers, lakes and litter bins
lampposts and benches
there might be fairies
there are magic mushrooms
I want round trees not pointed ones
playgrounds, camping and fire pits
more wildlife
flowers and gazebos
spiders
lighting on the trails
no litter
natural trees
we want a youth club
we need jobs for the kids
lighted trails and safety for people walking at night
I want a cabin to escape to in the woods
stuff to do that will make more people want to go up the hill
(people are stopping us)
we are generous, we are caring
litter bins, lampposts, flowers and ducks
a place to be buried overlooking my town
move the mountains and let the sunshine in
and there might be wolves . . .

What we found . . .
Every community is different. Different history, different personalities, and different levels of experience of managing community projects. The process must be flexible enough to adapt to each situation.

A successful community land project will require leadership from within the community. Those leaders, committed to making it happen, may already be identified or they may slowly emerge through the landscape design process.

All three of our communities had no difficulty in instinctively balancing the goals of the Well-being of Future Generations Act. Jobs and business opportunities were important but so were resilient ecosystems and the delivery of social and cultural benefits. There was no suggestion of focusing on one goal (for example, low-carbon income or jobs) at the expense of others.

In each of the communities, the older age group fully embraced the challenge of envisioning a landscape for the next three generations, a landscape they would never see.

The dream of the future . . .

We took the dreams and ideas from across the community and distilled a number of clear proposals that would be the starting point, the wish list for the first 10 years of community stewardship. Some are fully sustainable business operations; others are purely for community benefit. These are just a few of the ideas that were developed – each informed by expertise from commercial and social entrepreneurs and ecologists.

- *200-hectare [500-acre] natural woodland reserve*
- *Renewable energy generation from sunlight, water, and wood*
- *Forest crofts for families*
- *Commercial vegetable growing under glass on the old colliery site*
- *Community orchard and a pumpkin field*
- *Timber harvesting and processing operation*
- *Zero-carbon social housing*
- *Woodworking skills shed*
- *Treehouse glamping pods*
- *Forest performance space*
- *Green burial area . . .*

In all the time I've been a politician, and long before, there have been projects to create new opportunities in the South Wales valleys.

Learning

There is something fundamentally different about Skyline. This is not about communities having a project decided by others, applied to them. This is about communities galvanised into action by their own landscape. Once the final decision is made in each case about the land that will come under community stewardship, a long-term lease will be agreed and a community land trust will be established that gives control over the landscape to the community for the long term. Early in 2021 the journey to a more sustainable future will have begun. The destination will be under the control of the community that wants to build a place to meet the needs of both present and future generations.

What I love about Project Skyline is the way it is using the Act to galvanise new ideas within a responsible legal framework and thus encouraging new, different and more sustainable opportunities for future generations. On the one hand, it is very clearly about communities acting by and for themselves, but currently they don't own the land that this project needs, so that is where the government comes in – either to gift the land to the community if it is in government ownership or to facilitate by appropriate partnerships and planning conditions if it is not.

The Welsh Government's vision for Wales

My fundamental proposition, from the moment I started on my own journey, is that a government that is prepared to make decisions in the interests of current and future generations will make different and better decisions. That is why a clear statement from the the First Minister of Wales to that effect is so important.

Professor Mark Drakeford AM, First Minister of Wales, 2018–present
The United Nations Sustainable Development Goals are often described as 'ambitious', but surely that is not how they are best described. It is as if we were to describe the need for food, drink and sleep as ambitions of daily life. They are necessities and, if we

are serious about the future of the planet, its people and prosperity, these goals are fundamental.

That is the understanding we have in Wales and it is why we are committed to making our contribution to these global goals.

This is not just a commitment of the Welsh Government, but a historic commitment made by Senedd Cymru / the Welsh Parliament in 2015, in passing the Well-being of Future Generations (Wales) Act 2015. This signalled our commitment to a new contract between current and future generations, ensuring that no one is held back and reflecting Wales' great history of collective action to solve common problems.

The Act is built around a number of shared well-being goals for the future that are integrated and indivisible, eroding distinctions, and creating connections between justice in our economy, our society, our environment, and importantly for Wales, our language and culture.

People across Wales were engaged and mobilised through a national conversation on 'The Wales We Want in 2050'. The obligation to promote sustainable development was extended to public bodies across the whole of Wales – making it their central organising principle.

The Act established the world's first statutory independent Future Generations Commissioner to be an advocate for the long-term and support sustainable development in Wales.

Sustainable development means both doing things differently and doing different things – looking to the future; integrating the four dimensions of sustainable development; collaborating to find and deliver long-term solutions; preventing problems from occurring or getting worse; and finding new ways to involve people in the decisions that affect them, giving them ownership of the solutions and of the future.

At the heart of the Act lies the unifying goal of creating a 'More Equal Wales'. More equal societies do better economically and enjoy better health and well-being. They teach us that what matters to

Learning

us and our families is closely aligned with others; out of this we create the bonds of cohesive communities. Equality creates bonds between people just as inequality erodes them. A more equal Wales forms the basis of our determination to leave Wales and the world better than we found them. We don't inherit this fragile planet from the people who have come before us, we borrow it from those people who come after us and the Act puts that recognition at the forefront of practical actions.

Our approach to sustainable development is unique to Wales, formed from our history and international outlook. We are determined that Wales will become a nation powered by renewable energy as we strive to reduce emissions and hit our decarbonisation targets. The first industrial revolution began in the valleys of South Wales, before spreading around the world. Now we are determined to be at the forefront of the green revolution – investing in wind, wave and water energy sources. Our ambitions for zero waste, zero-net carbon and living within the planet's resources are a key part of this approach.

That is why I believe passionately that, as a globally responsible nation, our most radical days are ahead of us. A prosperous, resilient, healthier, more equal and globally responsible Wales, with cohesive communities and a vibrant culture and thriving Welsh language, is within our grasp and the Future Generations Act shows us the way.

The Well-being of Future Generations Act will be successful when we no longer need it.

CALVIN JONES, Professor of Economics,
Cardiff Business School

I am writing this as I sit in my Sydney home, literally surrounded by the greatest fire catastrophe the world has known. To me, the immediate and thoughtful adoption of legislation like the WFG Act in Wales is an essential move for offering younger generations some hope that there is a powerful leadership role for them to play in shaping society, fixing the wealth disparity and surviving the climate crisis.'

Leith Sharp, director and lead faculty,
Executive Education for Sustainability Leadership,
Harvard T.H. Chan School of Public Health

'With a carbon tax on all products reflecting the ecological destruction the product causes – their true cost – we can face destructive capitalism head on and implement the polluter-pays principle that should be common sense. The profits from the carbon tax should be returned to the people.'

Uffe Elbæk, member of Danish Parliament;
founder, Danish Green Party The Alternative
and former Danish Minister of Culture

'Within its very name, the Well-being for Future Generations Act embodies principles found within Indigenous Knowledges. When brought together, they mark the way to a future where decisions are based on positive relationships with the natural world. Indigenous resurgence around the world together with the leadership of the Welsh people are charting a course for the well-being of all who are here now and generations to come based on sustaining the world of which we are a part.'

Jane Gray, who worked on sustainability policies
for governments in Canada and internationally

CHAPTER 6

Loving

Wild Ideas for Wales and
the Wider World

*The sustainability revolution will have to be, above all, a
collective transformation that permits the best of human
nature, rather than the worst, to be expressed and nurtured.*

DONELLA MEADOWS

When I came to live where I live now, one of our greatest
joys was to find ourselves stewards of a small woodland
that had not been touched for nearly half a century. The
trees are a very British mix: mostly broadleaf with ash as the dominant
species and a huge number of self-seeded wild cherries with their
wonderfully, richly red-brown-coloured trunks, particularly after the
rain. There are oaks whose roots must have been laid in the time of the
industrial revolution and where some branches are now embedded as
lintels and windowsills in our refurbished barn home. There is a stand
of larch from which we have built our garage and wooden outbuild-
ings. What there was not, was a chestnut; neither horse chestnut for
conkers or a sweet chestnut for its fruit – despite chestnut trees being
able to live up to 800 years.

One of the first things we did when we moved in was to plant two
of each from local stock. City friends asked us why we were planting
trees that we would not see bear fruit. We answered that our children

and grandchildren would. In essence, the Act of planting a tree which should outlive you and your children can be called 'cathedral thinking', where long-term goals require decades of foresight and planning so future generations can enjoy their realisation. Legislating for future generations is 21st-century cathedral thinking. We should all be doing our own little bit of that.

Ideas for our future

My doctor father and I once had a discussion about whether people were inherently good or inherently bad. He thought it was safer to consider they were inherently bad and then be pleased when it was not the case. I thought it was better to assume the opposite because that's the kind of world I want to live in.

My experience in writing this book has borne out my optimism. There have been such a large number of people from all walks of life who've wanted to contribute, full of ideas of how to create a better Wales or a better world – a world that is fairer and healthier, where communities feel strengthened and where nature is restored. You will have heard many of these voices and their ideas throughout this book (their voices can be found in full at www.janedavidson.wales). I want to finish with a few loving, imaginative, collaborative ideas for Wales and the world, from people wishing us well on our journey and standing ready to advise, support and celebrate. I only wish my father were still alive to have that discussion with him today.

I begin with Carwyn Jones AM, First Minister of Wales, 2009–2018:

> There are some who will argue that sustainability is fine, as long as it doesn't impede economic growth. They see it as a burden to be tolerated. It's no burden to have jobs that last, communities that are balanced and vibrant, and an environment that's clean for people to appreciate.
>
> Sustainability creates jobs. From the wind turbines generating clean energy, from the tidal lagoons that can provide electricity

for over a century to the circular economy with jobs provided in recycling, the message has to be that sustainability is a long-term job creator, not a ball and chain around the economy.

There are exciting times ahead, and I'm proud that Wales has shown the way.

VOICES OF HOPE: THE DREAMERS

The 'Voices of Hope' that follow are those of the citizen dreamers – the citizens who have a vision for Wales which we should help deliver. Some have international reputations or are household names – Michael Sheen, Owen Sheers and Iolo Williams, for example. All of them have souls invested in Wales.

Michael Sheen OBE, actor and UNICEF ambassador

Let us be simple.

Let us attend to the basics.

Let us ensure that those who are without a home are helped to have and keep one. Those who are punished for their lack are protected from exploitation.

Those who suffer are supported.

No future can 'be' well if these basic needs cannot be met.

Simple but not easy.

Basic but too easily avoided.

Communities with the resources to define and solve their own challenges themselves. That is sustainability.

Communities with easy access to accurate information about themselves.

Communities where those in authority are held to account.

Communities where the voices of those without power are expressed, heard and acted upon.

#futuregen

We are a nation that has been plundered, divided, and disconnected for too long. The future must be one where we speak
through our own mouths not through the mouths of others.
Where our diverse histories can be the source of our strength,
not the fissures that keep us apart.
We must be wary of letting the frustration of our restrictions
and meagre self-determination become channelled into
making grand claims of ultimately toothless frameworks.
Of dancing round the edges, but acting like we're in the middle
of the dance floor.
All the will in the world is worthless without action.
So let us be simple and do whatever it takes to ensure our
future generations have the basics, remembering that our
present generations do not.
Simple but not easy.
Basic but too easily avoided.

Owen Sheers, Welsh poet and author

Term

At twenty eight weeks we conjured you again suspended in
parts in each dark frame
of one long, concertinaed ream.
A profiled skull, a snub-nosed mask
a skeleton palm held up against glass a marionette's leg of
fibula and femur.
A vision of which our parents never dreamt the bones of the
future in the present.
So why was it only weeks later
I finally took the time to look? What can I say?
There's always a reason not to pay attention you're our second
and here's a hard first lesson – there's something about the
adult brain

Loving

a curse a gift
I'll let you choose which
that can't sustain the marvellous for long.
But then
as if in answer to these thoughts
you offered up halfway down that chain flesh not bone
your lips and nothing else adrift in all that dark
pale and parted
as if to ask a question from the womb but also somewhere
    further on
when you'll be fully grown.
I stand in our kitchen
the window black with night
staring at your unborn mouth
open as if for breath
and can't help but wonder
to what degree will the question on your lips
be weighted with admiration or with anger? In what measure
    thanks or blame?
What phrase might it contain
to describe these years of squander?
And if
god help us
it should be specific – ask what it was we did where we stood
    and what we said
will we my daughter
have lived a good enough answer?

Iolo Williams, naturalist and TV wildlife presenter

The third *State of Nature* report reiterated the fact that our
wildlife is in a perilous state. One key factor in reversing

this decline is re-diverting agricultural grants from further intensification to serious wildlife payments with a high level of monitoring. This one action, if done properly, would go a long way to restoring our biodiversity.

Environmental pollution in all its forms must be addressed, with hefty fines for repeat offenders, and environmental education. Outdoor education and teachings about the natural world should be at the heart of the lessons being delivered in our schools. All lessons, from maths to art, chemistry to French, could benefit from being undertaken outside the classroom.

Education from primary levels should include key topics such as sustainability, conservation and ecology and I would urge the introduction of a GCSE in Natural History. Gone are the days when all children spent their weekends and school holidays outside and gone too are the basic wildlife identification skills that were common to every child.

I would love to see Wales lead the way in this field and to be the envy of the world with its all-inclusive wildlife education and healthy, living environment. I see the WFG Act as a real opportunity to push this forward. We can wait no longer.

Tim Jackson, ecological economist and playwright

In the incessant and tumultuous demands of today, why should we bother to care about tomorrow? I believe there are two main reasons. The first is justice. Justice for our children. Justice for other species. Blindingly obvious, obviously utopian and fiendishly difficult to achieve. That's why the Act is so important. 'I speak for the trees, for the trees have no tongues' said Dr Seuss' most famous character, the Lorax, in a book for future generations written half a century ago. The Well-being of Future Generations Act is the Lorax. It speaks for tomorrow because tomorrow has no voice. The second reason is more

Loving

surprising. It creeps up on us surreptitiously. It begins at home with our children. It extends itself to our friends and our colleagues. It builds from a sudden empathy for a fleeing refugee, a dying animal, a lost cause. It swells into a concern for the suffering of others that we cannot even properly articulate and often try to deny. But in denying it, we end up denying ourselves. Without this distressing, turbulent, raucous emotion, we are nothing. 'A society grows great when old men plant trees under whose shade they will never sit.' The Act is a device to enable our society to grow great.

Barbara Adam, Professor Emerita, Cardiff University, author of *Future Matters* and poet

Well-being of Future Generations Act – Unfulfilled Potential
The Act is focused on space and matter with time thus far the unrealised potential
Assumptions, mind-sets and strategies are bounded by this dual perspective
Time has the potential to turn the Act into a powerful change agent
inspiring collective imaginations to soar to unexpected heights
No longer from and for the present the Act expands
to encompass the future as on-going process
Facts, targets and indicator measures
recede from strategy dominance
Actions are tied to potential impacts
As they ripple across time, space & matter
Duty, obligation & responsibility become expanded
suitable to the reach of actions and their potential dispersals
The meaning of 'generations' is opened out appropriate to context
the number of encompassed generations relative to the situation involved
And 'well-being' gets tied to the beauty and power of the landscape that is Wales

My notes on 'The Future'
Dispelling myths about the future: The future is *not*
Open

#futuregen

An empty space
Ours to be colonised
A container to be filled
Separable from past and future
Something to be predicted (only)

Rather, we ought to be thinking of the future as
restricted as past delimits future options (path-dependence,
　　grandfathering, et cetera)
every present future-making action inserted into crowded,
　　delimited realm
& affects all that had been set on its course:
　　inter-connected/dependent
not separable from past and present which feature in future
a *crowded* space filled with past & present deeds
owned by successors, we are trespassers
as on-going reshuffling *processes*

Making distinctions
Present future
= is from and for the present, asking what can the future
　　do for us
Future present
= is standpoint of the future, concerned with potential
　　outcomes/effects of present actions on recipients, which
　　are possibly no yet born

Mark McKenna, co-founder/director, Down to Earth Project, Swansea

Imagine a Wales which is founded on principles of equality for
people and the natural world – a Wales which understands we
cannot thrive or close the gap in inequality until we develop a

Loving

new way of living which doesn't just have a 'neutral' impact on energy consumption or the natural world but which actively enhances biodiversity, improves air and water quality, increases topsoil and generates surplus energy.

Imagine what our children would say then . . . they would look back and the WFG Act would be the pivot point for creating a world where future generations have hope.

Andy Fryers, director of sustainability, Hay Festival

Generating a Future for Wales: A Mini-Manifesto
Looking forward and imagining a future where there is a future

Within 5 years
- The WFG Act has recognition and is understood by all the people of Wales, not just those who are charged with implementing it.
- The WFG Act is taught in schools within a curriculum that educates all pupils about modern political, social and environmental knowledge.
- Every private sector contract with the public sector has been reviewed and a plan produced for bringing it in line with WFG Act.
- A New Green Deal has been legislated for and is the blueprint for an economic, environmental and social revival.

Within 10 years
- The WFG Act has been used to build a platform for reform of the agricultural, fisheries, energy, technology, housing, health and transport sectors.

- The New Green Deal is providing sustainable jobs that provide both income and purpose, and allow flexible working with equal pay.
- Wales is leading the field and exporting its knowledge and experience to help other countries achieve incremental improvements.

Within 25 years
- Wales is a carbon negative country.
- Social justice and environmental consciousness is seen as more important than pure financial achievement.
- Wales is no longer seen as leading the field because every other country has also achieved parity.

Bill Hamblett, co-founder, Small World Theatre

It does not surprise me that Wales became the first country in the world to legislate for future generations. Many people ran away from the unthinking rapacious consumerism and irresponsible capitalism embodied in the cities and sought a new start in the West Wales' alternative movement.

Unfortunately, the power of the individual has been steered to reside almost exclusively in the power of the consumer, not the voice of people informing politics, coming through radical processes like Legislative Theatre. The individual also is allowed to seek the somewhat contradictory aspiration to 'make a difference'. We have 'made a difference', a negative and destructive difference, to the environment resulting in future generations with less of a choice and fewer resources. The Act now shows a way to make a *positive* difference and to hold to account those institutions that do not. Time is short. No less than the well-being of future generations.

Loving

Right now, very unfortunately and through no fault of their own, Welsh farmers have become commodity slaves, producing and selling food to remote and centralised markets, as a result of which their capacity to derive an adequate living from the land and to play their part in a vibrant community and food culture has been utterly compromised. In tandem with this, the majority of food that is sold in Wales is no longer produced in the principality, as a result of which public health has been dramatically undermined, and the sense of connectedness with the land through farming and food, which used to be the birthright of all Welsh citizens, has been compromised. It follows from all this that the health and well-being of future generations is completely dependent on rebuilding relocalised and resilient sustainable food systems from the ground up.

Justina Muhith, senior operations manager
at a pharmaceutical company, with an
imaginative law proposal

Whereby one area could not be overpopulated by a certain industry. There would be quotas allowed per city based on its population size as to how many restaurants could be introduced per population, how many private companies, how many pharmaceutical companies et cetera. If there were a more equal way to distribute types of businesses across the country, then there would be more chance of work (skilled and unskilled) as every geography would have a share of every industry. Raising the chance of keeping their local graduates, more financial contribution to the local economy,

reduced differences in living costs between regions of the
country, greater chances of enhancing the infrastructure
and public services for most areas of the U.K. over time.
Ultimately it would improve job prospects and give youngsters
confidence that they can progress in life whatever part of the
U.K. they live in!

There would be fewer pockets of under-educated or unem-
ployed people across the country. More areas would become
desirable to work in and live in.

Westminster devolves to the regions, but they need to help
us build a self-sustainable economy too . . .

Meena Upadhyaya,
Distinguished Honorable Professor,
Division of Cancer and Genetics, Cardiff University

I will make certain that children are introduced to multicul-
turalism as soon as they begin school, so that they learn to
integrate, accept difference or become more tolerant. I would
scrap all tuition fees for higher education. It is unfair and
encourages a divisive society, back to a class segregation, where
students from non-affluent backgrounds end up with debt.
We need a fairer society, one where the commercial interests
promote the well-being of society; at a minimum we should
start with bringing the Equality Act 2010 to life. Ten years in
waiting is already too little, too late!

Fern Smith, director, Emergence

The future is another country – if only Wales' legislation were
at the heart of this other country. It would be a great place in
which to live.

VOICES FROM ELSEWHERE

These are voices from those outside Wales – some of whom are looking to Wales for an example of leadership, others of whom are thinking about what this might mean in their own circumstances. I gave people permission to dream – what would be the primary purpose of an act that explicitly benefitted future generations? What action in their view would keep future generations more safe and secure? I am delighted at the imagination, common sense and achievability of the proposals. This is after all about crafting a better future, one in which we live in harmony with nature and recognise our responsibilities and opportunities to be better stewards for this single planet of ours.

Caroline Lucas, Green Party MP, U.K.

I'm delighted to be working with Lord Bird on the Future Generations Bill, building on the pioneering work in Wales which has already helped to embed longer-term sustainable thinking in the Welsh Government. While Lord Bird introduces the bill in the House of Lords, I'm planning to steer it through the House of Commons.

Identifying one single law that would most benefit future generations, however, has been a real challenge. I've decided to choose neither economic reform nor democratic renewal, vital though they are – but something closer to home and to my heart: a new law that would make mandatory the teaching of natural history in our schools. This echoes one of the demands of the school climate strikers: to reform the education system to teach young people about the urgency, severity and scientific basis of the climate crisis. But I believe it needs to go further than this – we need to be engendering a love for nature, not just instilling knowledge about the threats to it.

#futuregen

Kath Dalmeny, chief executive, Sustain, the U.K.'s alliance for better food and farming

There is now a growing and inspiring movement behind the concept of a 'Right to Food'. If we decided to instate this into law, this would be a game-changing legal and cultural framework that we could be rightly proud of gifting to our children and grandchildren. The Right to Food could catalyse action by governments, local authorities, businesses and civil society to ensure that food is produced sustainably and is fairly distributed, for the benefit of food producers and citizens alike.

True food security is not only about households being able to afford food. It is also about everyone being able to hold decision-makers to account for looking after the natural systems that provide our food – this most basic of human needs. A legal Right to Food could also trigger systematic support for our soils, pollinators, clean water and the large-scale shift to agro-ecological production that is now so urgently needed.

Tessa Clarke, co-founder and CEO, OLIO

Governments should legislate to optimise for the maximal 'well-being' of the nation rather than for GDP growth. Governments must promptly remove subsidies from the fossil fuel industry and rapidly deploy them towards clean energy. Next, businesses must become legally responsible for the full lifecycle of their products, meaning that customers no longer 'buy' things, but instead 'rent' them. The fiduciary responsibility of businesses should also be re-written to give equal weight to people, profit and planet in all decision making, rather than purely maximising shareholder returns. And finally to households, I would apply a 'pay as you throw' tax to all categories of product not covered by the manufacturer lifecycle legislation, so that we're forced to profoundly rethink our relationship with 'stuff'.

Laline Paull, author of *The Bees* and *The Ice*

Nurture not nature

Researching honeybee society, I was surprised to learn that the queen is made by nurture, not nature. Every single female egg that the queen lays has the innate biological potential to develop into a queen bee: it all depends how it is nourished. Nurture not nature makes a queen bee instead of a worker and a good education makes a perceptive and empowered citizen.

How many homeless people or people using foodbanks or those of in the swelling young prison population have had the benefit of the best education money can buy? And how many charity dinners with generous tax deductible donations in aid of ending homelessness, poverty and youth crime, are attended by those who did?

Where there is a monarchy there is a social hierarchy – the tiny privileged elite at the top and the vast majority at the bottom. We still have a queen, but we are not honeybees. Every child will benefit from good nutrition and a good education. If this country is home to all children born here and not just those of the rich and those who would be their willing serfs, then level the playing fields of the educational system. Abolish fee-paying schools, share the privilege of a good education with every single child and see how great Britain can truly be.

That is what I would want to see legislation for future generations achieve – state run, free and fair education for all.

Endnote
My Journey to Living Lightly

One of Donella Meadows' more trenchant remarks was, 'You may be able to fool the voters, but not the atmosphere', and it's hard to argue that we are not seeing the consequences of that writ large at the moment. Wanting to bring about a more sustainable world was not for her (or for me) a sacrifice, but an adventure, a journey to a better world than we have today; a world which does not suggest that our non-material needs – identity, community, self-esteem, love, joy – can be met by buying more stuff. This is another fundamental reset I'm advocating; what part can politics and government play in that?

I remain a strong believer in evidence-led policy, so the conscious realisation that the actions I take as an individual as well as those I contribute towards collectively can make the lives of future generations worse is an absolute nightmare. For me the political has always been personal and the personal, political. I am a conviction politician and policy maker. I cannot promote what I do not believe in. What became abundantly clear to me in 2007 was that I could not continue to be part of the problem. As a human being and as a minister, how could I promote a different lifestyle if I wasn't prepared to live it myself?

Having the responsibility of leading the government agenda on successfully living with only one planet available to us meant that I needed to consider not only policies to address that, but also what I was prepared to do in my own life. Since the key areas are related to food, buildings, transport, products, services, energy, resources and our lifestyles, I needed to make changes in all of these I could, as a politician, as a citizen and as a mum.

#futuregen

As a minister, I decided immediately not to fly unless it was absolutely necessary for my portfolio responsibilities – which meant I undertook some very long train journeys! Ironically, despite the inconvenience, the cost was always substantially greater to take trains and I continually had to argue the case, even within a government committed to sustainable development.

As a family, we decided to take at least one action to be greener every year, something we are still doing now; actions such as changing to a renewable energy supplier, cycling to work one day a week, using public transport wherever possible, not flying for holidays, buying local produce in season. These actions, which we started in 2007, led us by 2011 to move away from a single-glazed, badly insulated house with gas central heating to live on our smallholding with two fields and a woodland to keep us warm, in a well-insulated house, using energy from the sun, Earth and our woodland to power our lives (including creating our hot water and heating,) growing as much of our own food as possible (including honey and cider) and driving an electric car.

I can honestly say that this journey of ours to live lighter on the planet, contrary to the perceived wisdom of 'sackcloth and ashes', has been the absolute opposite. We have embarked on a wonderful adventure: adding purpose has improved the quality of our lives and our well-being, the more we consider what choices we make and why. We have met extraordinary people along the way who provide collective support and with whom we swap goods and services. We eat food grown without pesticides fresh from our land; we see on a daily basis the contrast between our organic holding and the wildlife-free, intensively farmed fields that surround us. Our lives and our land become richer as we carry on our annual commitment of being greener than the year before, not least because we are consciously acting in the interests of our and others' children and their children. We are trying to become part of the solution rather than part of the problem. Surely that is the least each one of us should do.

I'm acutely aware that the actual lifestyle choices we've made as a family are not available to the majority of people who live in cities, or whose lives are governed by the lack of money. I can also tell you from experience, it is very hard work and we will need in time to pass the baton on to younger, fitter people! But adding purpose to your life not to be part of the problem is a choice available to everyone. Recognising the damage we are doing to nature, individually and collectively, and changing our behaviour accordingly is a choice we can all make – and in Wales we can now make those demands of our government and our public services to help us deliver local solutions.

In *Beyond the Limits*, Donella describes three mental models to help us think about our behaviour, individually and collectively. Only one is hopeful, envisioning a better world. When faced with such a stark choice, what kind of world do you want to live in?

> *The world for all practical purposes has no limits.* This model
> allows extractive industries to extract and the human economy
> goes further beyond limits. The result is collapse
>
> *The limits are real, but there is not enough time.* People
> cannot be moderate, responsible or compassionate in time, so
> the model is self-fulfilling. The result is collapse.
>
> *The limits are real and close, but there is no time to waste.*
> There is just enough energy, enough material, enough money,
> enough environmental resilience and enough human virtue to
> bring about a planned reduction in the ecological footprint of
> humankind; a sustainability revolution to a much better world
> for the vast majority.

It's your choice, but when you make it, make it consciously, recognising that the choices each of us makes will have profound impacts well beyond our own lifetimes.

Thank you for reading this book.

Postscript

This book is being published at an extraordinary time. Across much of the world, COVID-19, an invisible killer, is stalking our lives – and our way of life. The response has been global, but neither planned nor coordinated, and we are all rapidly redefining what is really important in our lives. The threat of a pandemic was a known one. The U.K. Government held a national pandemic flu exercise, codenamed 'Exercise Cygnus', in October 2016 that identified that there were inadequate numbers of ventilation machines. No action was taken. There was no long-term thinking, no looking at the global regulation of markets, no recognition that global travel not only contributes to climate change but facilitates the rapid spread of infection.

In the interests of future generations, when this threat is over, there will be an opportunity to capitalise on our rediscovered kindness and sense of society, to celebrate the importance of nature, to build on our increased virtual engagement to act on that other silent killer – climate change – for the benefit of current and future generations. We know now that governments can act – and quickly – when faced with an emergency that they must address. We must next encourage them to respond similarly to the existential threats of climate change and nature degradation to current and future generations. And #futuregen is one path open to them.

In the meantime, our gratitude goes out to those who have kept us safe, fed and cared for: those in emergency services, the care workers, the medical teams, the postal workers, the shelf stackers, the refuse collectors, the food producers and distributors. We salute you.

March 2020

The Last Word

by Sophie Howe, Wales' first Future Generations Commissioner

When I was asked by Jane to contribute 'the last word' for this book, I was of course interested. So much has been said about the Act, from its conception to what it's achieved so far, and yet how does anyone have the last word on something like the Well-being of Future Generations Act, something that still feels so in its infancy?

I have been in the post as Wales' first Future Generations Commissioner since 2016. During that time it's fair to say I've talked about future generations with just about everyone I've met, from global leaders to the people living in our communities in Wales, to chief executives of businesses and to my local hairdresser.

Protecting the interests of future generations has officially gone mainstream. No longer niche issues, confined to the bowels of the UN or environmental lobby groups, intergenerational justice and climate change are in our Twitter feeds, in editorials in teen magazines, conversations at the school gates and Netflix television series.

It's something that no matter where you are you can have an opinion on. No matter what your political affiliation or opinions, the one thing that unites us all is our collective interest in and our right to a future – to a tomorrow.

We have made quite a splash with our Well-being of Future Generations Act as the first country in the world to make such a law – and brave enough to do so. I can see that there is a growing movement of change, with people who believe in improving the social, cultural, environmental and economic well-being of Wales and are daring to deliver differently within their own organisations and wider, often amidst a backdrop of political uncertainty and continued austerity.

But I am realistic that while many talk of a journey to implementation, what we are actually embarking on is more of an expedition. Something you must have the bravery for, the tools for and a determination to do difficult things, things that have not been done before.

Across Wales I am seeing the legislative framework inspire and deliver on each of these aspects, but this is usually without then seeing all of these things as essential, integrated parts of bringing about long-term change.

I am seeing individual champions of the Act and its ways of working change the way transport planning is being done in our capital city, taking a public-health approach, reforming the way we think about keeping older people well, shifting beyond delivering 'services' to focusing on what matters to them.

I'm seeing politicians reject the status quo of addressing congestion by building more roads and instead looking for solutions that will be better for the well-being of people and planet.

I'm seeing the framework of the law driving contracting decisions so that investment in our new rail contract will also help to tackle poverty through provision of cheaper fares in more disadvantaged areas as well as use a supply chain of social enterprises and clean energy sourced in Wales.

I am seeing national policy change to support well-being, with place-making being the core principle in how we plan design and build communities. I'm seeing the roll-out of a new education curriculum in which young people will be supported to be creative, enterprising and ethnically informed citizens.

But I'm also seeing gaps in implementation and the need for a more coherent approach to implementing the Act at every level and through an equal focus on policy, process and people. Often where good things are happening, they appear to be pieces of a jigsaw that don't always fit into the wider puzzle of the organisational approach.

The Last Word

We are dealing with a new way of working within the Well-being of Future Generations Act that is often at odds with a raft of existing and, unfortunately, occasionally new policy legislation and guidance. My office is working alongside the government to wade through this, working on reform and alignment.

In some areas we are seeing how brilliant organisations are using the Act, not just to do the same thing better, but to do better things. However, this is not always recognised and driven by the corporate centre of these organisations – a disjointedness between strategy and action. And on the flip side of that, I have seen organisations more focused on the process than the wider cultural change, with a lack of support and resources to help people shift from old to new ways of thinking.

As one of my statutory duties as Commissioner, this year I am publishing the first Future Generations Report. The report provides an assessment of the progress made to date and provides advice on improvements public bodies should make in order to set and meet well-being objectives.

It will say that we need to increase the pace of progress on decarbonisation, that we need to change the way we view the financing of our health care system towards keeping people well rather than treating them when they're ill. It will commend the efforts the government is making on well-being budgeting, while encouraging it to go further, and it will say clearly that progressive and game-changing laws like this must have greater support for implementation on the ground.

Throughout the remainder of my term, I will continue to support and challenge, and be stronger in my approach to public bodies who are failing to implement the transformational changes needed.

Sometimes, when people talk about the future, it seems to be all automation and robots. They seem to think there's some technological silver bullet that will solve all our issues. Maybe, one day, that might become a reality, but that's not where I get my hope for the future from.

I will continue to take hope on a daily basis from the growing number of people, communities and organisations who individually are making sometimes simple and small changes. The smaller projects

#futuregen

I hear about, the people who have used the requirements of the Act as a prompt or tool to get an initiative off the ground because they know it's the right thing to do. The people who see a different way of doing things and are unafraid to call out those with their blinkers on. The people I like to refer to as the 'frustrated champions'. There are many in our public sector in Wales, but they're often in all walks of life.

I'm sure you've met a frustrated champion in your time. Perhaps you even are one. They're the people who walk the talk. The mum who campaigns for a ban on plastic straws in the school. The civil servant who rewrites a procurement policy despite constant opposition and barriers. The teenager who writes to their local Assembly Member to question how the government is responding to the climate emergency. The minister who won't take no for an answer and helps to make this legislation a reality.

This won't be the last word on the Well-being of Future Generations Act. It will keep going as long as there are enough of those frustrated champions out there to keep working towards a better future; enough of those frustrated champions out there agitating, ruffling feathers, speaking truth to power and challenging leaders to make it a reality.

We're building a movement for change here in Wales that will echo throughout the rest of the world. We want to ensure that there is no last word when it comes to our future generations.

ACKNOWLEDGEMENTS

This book would not have happened without the extraordinary generosity of others – in particular, those who gave freely of their time reading the early chapters to confirm the accuracy of my content and timeline – Andrew Charles, Alun Netherwood, Jessica McQuade, Sue Pritchard, Andy Middleton and Peter Davies – although my interpretation is very much my own. Heartfelt thanks to you all.

My writing journey was made all the easier by the inspirational army of contributors who imagined what Wales – or indeed any country – might do differently if it put the needs of future generations at the heart of public policy and delivery. Their thoughts and ideas are in the book, but to hear from them directly, go to www.janedavidson.wales where their contributions appear in full under their own names. Read and learn.

I want to shout out to two people in particular I met through writing the book; to Jonathan Boston, professor of public policy at the Wellington School of Business and Government, New Zealand, and my new virtual best friend whose thoughtful influence is in every chapter of this book; also to Ella Robertson, the CEO of One Young World whose amazing team walked the conference floor of this extraordinary annual gathering of next-generation leaders from across the world and gave me voice contributions (featured in the last pages of this book), which are an extraordinary insight into young people's lives in other countries, many far less free than our own. There are opportunities galore here for ideas to shape a nation's future, and I thank you all for your input.

To Sophie Howe – a special thanks for contributing the last word. Similarly, to my previous cabinet colleagues for contributing their views then and now, and to Mark Drakeford, the current First Minister of Wales, for his determination to lead.

#futuregen

Deep gratitude to Jon Rae, my commissioning editor; to Muna Reyal, who graciously and patiently turned my rambling text into this book; and to all at Chelsea Green for a roller-coaster experience.

And of course, everlasting thanks to Guy and my wonderful family who have given me the space, the time and the never-ending cups of tea to make it happen.

'One Wales, One Planet'

Our Vision of Sustainable Wales

I n 2009, the then Welsh Government published 'One Wales, One Planet' – which subsequently underpinned 'The Wales We Want' consultation and was turned into law through the Well-being of Future Generations (Wales) Act.

The section of 'One Wales, One Planet' that people related to very positively was its vision of a sustainable Wales. Living more sustainably is a journey, but we all need an understanding of what the journey looks like and what the destination might look like too – an active reinvigoration of communities in harmony with nature; a country at the forefront of low-carbon prosperity and reaping the benefit, while celebrating and preserving our natural surroundings.

To know the vision that the legislation seeks to deliver, read on:

Across society there is recognition of the need to live sustainably and reduce our carbon footprint. People understand how they can contribute to a low-carbon, low-waste society, and what other sectors are doing to help. These issues are firmly embedded in the curriculum and workplace training. People are taking action to reduce resource use, energy use and waste. They are more strongly focused on environmental, social and economic responsibility, and on local quality of life issues, and there is less emphasis on consumerism. Participation and transparency are key principles of government at every level, and individuals have become stewards of natural resources.

#futuregen

We have strong, active, resilient and supportive communities where people take responsibility for their own actions and how they affect others. Wales is a bi-lingual society, is fairer and more equal, and there is a reduction in the gap between rich and poor. Employment levels are high, and people enjoy a greater work – life balance, with more opportunities for volunteering. People work closer to home.

Many communities are taking action locally to reduce emissions and have developed local carbon budget programmes. Action has been taken to ensure that reducing greenhouse gas emission and the impacts of climate change do not increase social exclusion in Wales. People are active in maintaining the quality of the local environment where they live.

Economic regeneration is undertaken with sustainable development at its core, and promotes low-carbon, low-waste ways of working. There has been a huge growth in businesses that supply the goods and services needed to support a sustainable economy, including within the third sector. This growth has been underpinned by the development of training and qualifications in key sectors and in key skills needed for the production of low-carbon, low-waste goods and services. Wales is home to a number of world-leading technology development companies and manufacturing plants. The emphasis is on durable, recycled, recyclable and re-usable goods, and goods which are low carbon. These products are used locally and exported. Much more freight is moved by rail.

The energy intensity of society has decreased significantly. There has been a consistent drop in energy and water demand. There has been a major increase in renewable energy generation, offshore and onshore. All remaining fossil fuel plants have much improved energy efficiency, use their waste heat productively, and have carbon capture and storage fitted.

Heavy industry and the power generation sector have greatly improved the energy efficiency of their processes and [are] reducing the embedded carbon in their products. Large, energy-intensive sites are maximising the productive use of waste heat and supplying other businesses and homes.

Waste – whether of energy or other resources is taboo – both from a cost and societal impact. There is less light pollution. Resources are valued and, as a result, there has been a huge reduction in waste production and a much greater emphasis on reuse. Composting and recycling are at very high levels, and the third sector is active in providing services to enable reuse and recycling.

Walking and cycling are much more commonplace. There is greatly enhanced provision for cyclists and pedestrians within towns and cities, with improved walking and cycling networks, as well as better street design and traffic management measures. There are fast, reliable, affordable public transport services connecting major settlements. There are frequent, reliable mass transit services within cities and more heavily urbanised regions. There is a coherent network of sustainable transport options within rural Wales. Travel Plans are part of all new developments. All employers develop and implement Travel Plans

The 'school run' has been replaced by organised school transport or group walking/cycling. Petrol and diesel prices remain high, engine efficiency has increased with the widespread take-up of hybrid vehicles. People buy smaller, more efficient cars, and lift-sharing is a common way of travelling. The carbon content of transport fuels has reduced. The rate of growth in air travel has slowed down and it is no longer regarded as a necessity.

Good-quality housing for all is the norm. Homes and businesses are far more energy efficient and sustainable – all existing buildings at least meet Energy Performance Certificate Standard C and many are on the way to becoming carbon neutral. All new buildings are constructed to the highest standards of energy and water efficiency and are zero carbon. New development and infrastructure are located, designed and constructed for the climate they will experience over their design life and to minimise travel needs.

#futuregen

The public sector has led the way in this area, and sustainable development is the central organising principle of public service. Public buildings, schools, further and higher education institutions, hospitals and community buildings have been early, visible demonstrators of greater energy efficiency and renewable technology. They have also pioneered staff and service delivery approaches that minimise the need to travel. Many services are available locally and IT is used extensively to connect to specialist services.

Sustainable development and global citizenship is firmly embedded into all levels of educational provision and lifelong learning in Wales, and all schools are eco- and fairtrade schools. Levels of educational attainment are high.

There is a much greater emphasis on preventative healthcare throughout society, and many more people are living healthy lives through eating better and getting exercise more regularly as part of their everyday lives. Increased localisation means that people are eating more seasonal, fresh, local produce. This has stimulated agriculture and horticulture in Wales and there is much greater consideration given to the provenance of food. Much more food is traded locally where possible and fairly with the developing world when not. There is a huge expansion in allotments and community gardening. The agricultural industry has adapted to a changing climate, including making provision for the impacts of warmer summers, and changes in land use and management.

Wales' historic landscapes have been preserved, and we have learnt lessons from our past which inform our future management. We are now also managing land for the wider ecosystem services it can deliver, including carbon storage, water quality, flood management and landscape quality and connectivity for wildlife to adapt to climate change. As a result, the loss of biodiversity has been halted and there is a greater number, range and genetic diversity of wildlife. There is a greater understanding and appreciation of our interdependence with the other species we share the planet with.

Appendix 1

The marine environment is managed sustainably on an ecosystem approach, and there is an ecologically coherent, representative and well-managed network of marine protected areas. Many more people enjoy sustainable access to enjoy the countryside and coast. Wales' historic environment and heritage is sustainably managed and is accessible to all, sustainable transport options for visitors are more commonplace, and this underpins Wales' brand as a sustainable tourism destination.

Wales is recognised internationally as a leader in sustainable development, and learns from, and exports its learning to, other small nations and regions in Europe and wider afield.

Useful Resources

The History of the Well-being of Future Generations (Wales) Act 2015

These pages provide web links to documents and statements that formed key parts of the development of the Well-being of Future Generations (Wales) Act 2015. This has been drafted by the Futures Team within the Welsh Government in response to queries from academia and others on the origins and development of the Act in Wales. The list below is not exhaustive.

1998–2009:
Devolution journey (sustainable development duty)
Government of Wales Act 1998 (see section 121)
https://law.gov.wales/constitution-government/devolution/gowa-98/

Government of Wales Act 2006 (see section 79, 'Sustainable Development', and section 60, 'Promotion etc. of Well-being')
https://law.gov.wales/constitution-government/devolution/gowa-06/
The above acts required the publication of a Sustainable Development Scheme.

#futuregen

First Sustainable Development Scheme
Learning to Live Differently: The Sustainable Development
Scheme of the National Assembly for Wales
http://www.senedd.wales/Laid%20Documents/Learning%20to%
20Live%20Differently%20-%20The%20Sustainable%20Development
%20Scheme%20of%20the%20National%20Assembly%20for
%20Wales-09112000-23880/bus-GUIDE-3A0BD19D0006E0AE
000061C900000000-English.pdf

Second Sustainable Development Scheme
Starting to Live Differently:
The Sustainable Development Action Plan 2004–2007
Webpage:
https://webarchive.nationalarchives.gov.uk/20080107224105
/http://new.wales.gov.uk/topics/sustainabledevelopment
/publications/startlivedifferently/?lang=en
Document:
https://webarchive.nationalarchives.gov.uk/20080107224131
/http://new.wales.gov.uk/topics/sustainabledevelopment
/publications/susdevactionplan/?lang=en

Third Sustainable Development Scheme
One Wales, One Planet: The Sustainable Development
Scheme, 2009
http://www.assembly.wales/Laid%20Documents/GEN-LD7521%20
-%20One%20Wales%20One%20Planet%20-%20The%20Sustainable
%20Development%20Scheme%20of%20the%20Welsh%20Assembly
%20Government-22052009-130462/gen-ld7521-e-English.pdf

One Wales, One Planet: Annual Report 2009–2010
http://www.assembly.wales/Laid%20Documents/GEN-LD8219
%20-%20One%20Wales%20One%20Planet%20-%20The
%20Sustainable%20Development%20Annual%20Report%202009
-2010-21092010-196494/gen-ld8219-e-English.pdf

Appendix 2

Sustainable Development and Business Decision Making
in the Welsh Assembly Government
(Wales Audit Office, 2010)
> http://www.audit.wales/publication/sustainable-development
> -and-business-decision-making-welsh-assembly-government

Effectiveness Review of the Sustainable Development Scheme:
A Report to Welsh Government (PwC, 2011)
> http://www.assembly.wales/Laid%20Documents/GEN-LD8769
> %20-%20Effectiveness%20Review%20of%20the%20Sustainable
> %20Development%20Scheme%20A%20Report%20to%20the
> %20Welsh%20Government-23012012-229674/gen-ld8769
> -e-English.pdf

2012–2016: Legislating for sustainable development
Programme for Government (Welsh Government, 2011)
This is where the commitment to legislate was made by the Welsh
Government with the aim to become a 'One Planet nation', putting
sustainable development at the heart of government. See Chapter 11
in the Programme for Government for the commitments relating to
the Sustainable Development / Well-Being of Future Generations Bill.

Proposals for a Sustainable Development Bill (May 2012)
> https://gov.wales/proposals-sustainable-development-bill

Sustainable Development White Paper (December 2012)
> https://gov.wales/sustainable-development-bill-white-paper
> https://gov.wales/sites/default/files/consultations/2018-01
> /121203asusdevwhitepaperen.pdf

Sustainable Development White Paper – Resource Pack
(December 2012)
> https://gov.wales/sites/default/files/consultations/2018-01
> /130222sustainable-development-resource-pack-en.pdf

#futuregen

The Wales We Want by 2050 – A Welsh Society's Commitment
to a Better Quality of Life for Future Generations
(Welsh Government, 2014)
>   https://gov.wales/written-statement-future-generations-bill-wales
>   -we-want-2050
A link to the full legislation is on the main U.K. legislation enacted website:
>   http://www.legislation.gov.uk/anaw/2015/2/contents/enacted

2014–2016: The National Conversation:
The Wales We Want
Website
>   http://www.cynnalcymru.com/project/the-wales-we-want/

Final Report
>   http://www.cynnalcymru.com/wp-content/uploads/2015/01
>   /TWWW-Report-FINAL.pdf

**Well-Being of Future Generations (Wales) Act pages on the
National Assembly for Wales**
>   http://business.senedd.wales/mgIssueHistoryHome.aspx
>   ?IId=10103

Explanatory Memorandum
This is a useful document that sets out the case for change and options.
>   http://www.assembly.wales/laid%20documents/pri-ld9831-em-r
>   %20-%20well-being%20of%20future%20generations%20(wales)
>   %20bill%20-%20revised%20explanatory%20memorandum/pri
>   -ld9831-em-r-e.pdf

Local Authorities and the Act
>   https://www.wlga.wales/local-authorities-and-the-future
>   -generations-act

Animation Introducing the Act
>   https://www.youtube.com/watch?v=rFeOYlxJbmw

Appendix 2

2016–Present:
Implementing the Act and putting in place the building blocks
Welsh Government web pages
https://gov.wales/well-being future-generations-wales-act
-2015-guidance

Well-being of Future Generations Act: The Essentials
https://gov.wales/sites/default/files/publications/2019-08/well
-being-of-future-generations-wales-act 2015 the essentials.pdf

Statutory Guidance
https://gov.wales/well-being-future-generations-wales act
-2015-guidance

National Indicators for Wales
https://gov.wales/national-wellbeing-indicators

2015–2016:
How Do You Measure a Nation's Progress? Consultation
https://gov.wales/well-being-future-generations-wales-act-2015
-how-do-you-measure-nations-progress
https://gov.wales/sites/default/files/consultations/2018-02
/151022-fg-act-consultation-document-en.pdf

Well-being of Wales: 2017 (statutory Annual Well-being Report)
https://gov.wales/well-being-wales-2017

Well-being of Wales: 2018
https://gov.wales/well-being-wales-2018

Wales' Indicators against the UN Sustainable Development Goals:
https://gov.wales/national-wellbeing-indicators
https://gov.wales/national-indicators-mapping-well-being-and
-un-sustainable-development-goals-interactive-tool

#futuregen

Measuring Our Nation's Progress:
Proposals for National Milestones (2019)
https://gov.wales/measuring-our-nations-progress

Future Generations Commissioner for Wales
The Future Generations Commissioner's office is the first port of call for a range of resources, reports, good-practice examples and commentary.
https://futuregenerations.wales

Future Generations Framework for the public sector and others
https://futuregenerations.wales/resources_posts/future
-generations-framework/

Auditor General for Wales
Reflecting on Year One
https://www.audit.wales/publication/reflecting-year-one

Reflections on the journey to the Act
(papers that we are aware of)
World Health Organization
Sustainable Development in Wales and Other Regions in Europe – Achieving Health and Equity for Present and Future Generations (2017):
http://www.euro.who.int/__data/assets/pdf_file/0007/354580
/wales-report-20171116-h1520-web.pdf

16th Conference IAOS (organised with OECD) (2018)
Paper submitted by the Welsh Government on 'How Welsh Statisticians Are Helping to Measure the Progress of a Nation':
http://www.oecd.org/iaos2018/programme/IAOS-OECD2018
_Jones-Leake-Charles.pdf

Network of Regional Governments for Sustainable Development:
Localizing the Sustainable Development Goals (2018)
https://www.regions4.org/

Appendix 2

The Elders on Safeguarding Future Generations (2019)
https://theelders.org/news/safeguarding-future-generations
-how-wales-leading-way-climate-justice

Jonathan Boston, professor of public policy at the Wellington School of Business and Government, New Zealand
'Foresight, Insight and Oversight: Enhancing Long-Term Governance through Better Parliamentary Scrutiny', written with David Bagnall and Anna Barry

https://www.victoria.ac.nz/ data/assets/pdf_file/0011/1753571
/Foresight-insight-and-oversight.pdf

Further Information
Regions4 Sustainable Development
The global movement of regional governments, of which Wales was a founding member, is a great resource, demonstrating action on the ground now in relation to climate change, biodiversity and sustainable development:

https://www.regions4.org

The RSA Food, Farming and Countryside Commission
Understanding what good can look like will be helped by the huge body of work carried out by the RSA, directed by a Welsh organic farmer, Sue Pritchard. The commission started its work following the Brexit vote to leave the EU in 2016. It identified that food, farming and countryside policies are currently too fragmented to progress far enough and fast enough to make the necessary changes. Agriculture policies are disconnected from health policy; environmental policy is disconnected from trade policy; social policies are disconnected from the industrial strategy. The commission's 2019 report has become the most downloaded report from the RSA in its history and is definitely worth a read:

https://www.thersa.org/action-and-research/rsa-projects
/public-services-and-communities-folder/food-farming-and
-countryside-commission

#futuregen

Morgan Parry Lecture
Downloads available here:
http://www.morganparry.cymru/
Here are direct links to Welsh and English versions:
http://www.morganparry.cymru/pdf/Cymru-yn-2050.pdf
http://www.morganparry.cymru/pdf/wales-in-2050-eng.pdf

Schumacher College
An internationally renowned learning community in south-west England, offering ecology-centred master's degrees, short courses linked to living sustainably and horticulture programmes. Started by Satish Kumar, the college was established to reflect the ideas of E.F. Schumacher, the economist who pioneered the idea 'Small is Beautiful'.
https://www.schumachercollege.org.uk

Climate Outreach
Their toolkit for Welsh narratives and images for sustainability and climate change is here:
https://climateoutreach.org/resources/
sustainable-development-narratives-for-wales
Their global environmental narratives project:
https://climateoutreach.org/resource-type/global-narratives

Project Skyline
https://skyline.wales

INDEX

A
accountability
    for sustainable development
        initiatives, 58–60
    WWF report on Wales, 61–62
Adam, Barbara, on conceptions
    of the future, 161–62
Agar, Kian, 100
Agenda 21 of Earth Summit,
    Rio de Janeiro, 19
agriculture
    biodiversity and, 160
    climate change and, 104
    health care and, 184
    for One Planet Developments
        (OPDs), 14, 115
    regenerative, 109, 144
    in second scheme, 42
    town centre regeneration
        and, 114
alternative energy generation
    Cardiff Airport and aviation
        fuel, 126
    fuels, in second scheme, 41
    homes as power stations, 119
    microgeneration of, 41
    Project Skyline, 147
    public buildings, in second
        scheme, 41

reuse of materials, 120–21
solar farms, 6, 118
South Wales and potential
    for, 5–6
Swansea Bay Tidal Lagoon,
    118
in transport, 119
wind power, 5–6
Area of Outstanding National
    Beauty, 4
Arthur, Mari, on vision for future,
    97–98
Attenborough, David, 145
Auditor General (AGW), 113–14

B
Balch, Oliver, 95
banking. See Circular Economy
    Wales credit system
Bates, Clive, 'One Wales, One
    Planet,' 55–58
Bees and the Ice, The (Paull), 169
Beyond the Limits (Meadows),
    20–21, 173
biodiversity, 112–13, 121. See
    also wildlife
Bird, Lord John, 22, 132–35, 167
    Future Generations Bill
        (U.K.), 132–33

Blake, Chris, 145–46
Boston, Jonathan, 105
    Foresight, Insight and Oversight, 91–92
Brexit, potential effects of, 129
Brundtland Report definition of sustainable development, 29, 33, 88, 89
Brundtland, Gro Harlem, 33
Building Research Establishment Environmental Assessment Method (BREEAM) standards, 41
Burgess, Evan, 100

C
Caerau and Project Skyline, 148
carbon footprint. *See* ecological footprint
Cardiff Airport, 126
Cardiff Coal Exchange, 4
Carmarthen Business School, 115–16
'cathedral thinking' for town centre planning, 114
Celtic language, 3–4. *See also* Urdd National Eisteddfod
Center for Ecoliteracy at Berkeley, 20
chastisement, ban on, 48
Children as Researchers methodology, 123
Children's Commissioner, 36, 92
Circular Economy Wales credit system, 98–99, 120–21
civil service, 60–61, 73–74

Clarke, Tessa, on GDP versus sustainable growth, 168–69
climate change
    acknowledged as threat to humanity, 47
    biodiversity and, 121
    education and, 99, 123
    in Future Generations Bill, 87, 91
    Greta Thunberg and, 105
    housing, energy efficient, 119
    Intergovernmental Panel on Climate Change, 135
    M4 Relief Road unfunded, 117
    National Assembly declaration, 128
    Transport for Wales and Metro plans, 118
    UN committees and reports, 134
    'The Wales We Want,' 85
Climate Change Act (U.K.), 131–32
Climate Change Champions, 122
Climate Change Commission, 78
Climate Justice Programme, 76
Climate Outreach, 96
Committee on Climate Change (U.K.), 134
communities, in first scheme, 35
Conference of Parties (COP 15), Copenhagen, 131
Convention on the Rights of the Child, 36

Index

COVID-19 and global
response, 174
Creating Enterprise modular
homes, 119
Crompton, Adrian (AGW), 114
Cross-Party Beer and Pub
Group, 82
Cross-Party Built Environment
Group, 82
Cross-Party Diabetes Group, 82
Cross-Party Healthy Living
Group, 82
Cuthbert, Jeff (Minister for
Communities and Tackling
Poverty), 82
cycling, for schoolchildren, 51
Cynnal Cymru—Sustain Wales,
34, 51, 53, 61, 83, 97

D
Dale, Helen, 123
Dalmeny, Kath, on 'Right to
Food,' 168
Davenport, Juliet, 8
Davidoff Report, 39
Davidson, Jane
  activism, in Thatcher
    era, 14
  anti-poverty work, 16–17
  childhood of, 9–14
  Deputy Presiding Officer of
    National Assembly, 32
  education of, 12–13
  Education, Lifelong Learning
    and Skills, 32, 44

Environment, Sustainability
  and Housing, 46–47
Funky Dragon of Children
  and Young's People Assembly for Wales, 36
home life, 103–4, 155–56, 174
Minister for Education,
  Lifelong Learning and
  Skills, 42–44, 72
Minister of Environment,
  Sustainability and Housing,
  46–47, 72
portfolio, as minister,
  47–50, 58
racism, early encounters
  with, 11–12
recycling efforts, 18
speech on laws for sustainability, 73–74
Thatcher era, 14
'Towards Zero Waste,' 12, 63
tree planting, 155–56
'Wales for Africa' fair trade,
  44–45
walking the Wales Coast
  Path, 17–18
Welsh Local Government
  Association, 17
Davies, Peter, 46, 53, 64, 83
Davies, Ron, 30
democracy, reframing philosophy
  of, 27
devolution for Wales, 29–30
Director General for Sustainable
  Futures, 55, 61

Down to Earth Project, 162–63
Drakeford, Mark (AM), 15,
  107, 113
  statement on the Act, 151–53

E
Earth Overshoot Day, 132
Earth Summit, Johannesburg, 37
Earth Summit, Rio de Janeiro,
  19, 27–28, 143
ecological footprint, reducing
  biodiversity enhancement,
    121
  EcoHomes, 42
  eight key sectors of, 49
  estimates of, 50
  housing, 119
  Labour Party manifesto,
    66–67
  lifestyle choices, 171–73
  M4 Relief Road, 116–17
  One Planet Developments
    (OPDs), 115
  personal choices, 49
  reducing, 13–14, 48–50,
    52, 153
  'Towards Zero Waste,' 12, 63
  transport, 119–20
economy
  ecology first, 141–43
  in first scheme, 35
  global financial crisis of
    2008, 132
  root of words 'economy' and
    'ecology,' 142

education
  biodiversity projects, 121
  Carmarthen Business School,
    115–16
  Center for Ecoliteracy at
    Berkeley, 20
  chastisement, ban on, 48
  climate change actions and
    reports, 134
  eco-schools, 47, 122
  Foundation Phase curricu-
    lum, 43–44
  global learning curriculum, 44
  outdoor learning, 43–44,
    160–61
  as part of second scheme, 42
  problems caused by
    poverty, 16
  role of universities, 116
  school meals, sustainable,
    42, 118
  Schumacher College, 142
  special needs of students, 16
  vision for future, 97
  Welsh Curriculum
    Authority, 44
  Young Leaders Academy, 122
Education and Lifelong
  Learning, 32
Education for Sustainable Devel-
  opment and Global Citizenship
  (ESDGC), 44, 45, 196
Education, Lifelong Learning and
  Skills, 36, 44, 72
Effectiveness Reviews, 7

Index

Elbæk, Uffe, 154
electric vehicles, 100, 118, 119, 123
Emergence, 166
Emerson, Ralph Waldo, 13
employment and 'Living Wage,' 117
energy. *See* alternative energy generation
'Energy We Want, The,' 84
Environment Act (Wales), 88, 125
Environmental Audit Committee (EAC), 29
environmental justice, 79–83
Environment, Sustainability and Housing brief, 46–47, 72
ESDGC: A Strategy for Action, 45
Essex, Sue (AM), 15, 16, 30–31
European Foundation for Environmental Education (FEE) Scheme, 122

F
fair trade and 'Wales for Africa,' 6, 44–45
Field Guide for the Future (Food, Farming and Countryside Commission), 118
food security, 97, 109
    Kath Dalmeny on, 168
    public procurement, 117–18
    school meals and local sources, 118
Food, Farming and Countryside, *Field Guide for the Future*, 118

Foot, Michael, 14
Foresight, Insight and Oversight (Boston), 91–92
Foundation Phase curriculum, 43–44
four dimensions/domains of well-being, 111
Friends of the Earth, 37, 73, 76, 80
Fryers, Andy, 54
    Generating a Future for Wales: A Mini-Manifesto, 163–64
Funky Dragon of Children and Young's People Assembly for Wales, 36, 122
Future Champions, 84, 86
Future Generations (U.K.) Bill, 84, 167
    expanding to U.K., 132–35
    seven foundations for, 85
Future Generations Commissioner, 87, 90, 92–94, 152
Future Generations Report, 177

G
gardening, GRAFT project, 121
Girardet, Herbert, 5–6
Government of Wales Act 1998, 26, 47–48
Gower Peninsula, 4
Gray, Jane, 154
Green Dragons' Den, 55
Green Gown Award, 116
Greening Government (U.K.), 29

Green New Deal, 164
Griffiths, John (AM), 78–79

H
Hamblett, Bill, on individuals
  making a difference, 164
Hay Festival launch of 'One
  Wales, One Planet,' 54–55
health
  challenges in Wales, 5
  in first scheme, 35
  Hywel Dda University Health
  Board, 120
  local foods, 117–18
  Public Health Wales, 120
  sustainable transport
  vehicles, 119
hiking
  Coity Tip Trail, 121
  Pembrokeshire Coast Path,
  12–13, 69–70
Holden, Patrick, on sustainable
  and local farming, 165
housing
  Creating Enterprise modular
  homes, 119
  EcoHomes, 42
  homes as power stations, 119
Howe, Sophie (Future Generations Commissioner), 93–94,
  110, 122, 175–78
Hughes, Medwin, 110, 116
Hutchins, Giles, 136
Hutt, Jane, 15
hydrogen car manufacturing, 118

Hywel Dda University Health
  Board, 120

I
Industrial Revolution in Wales, 130
Institute for Governance and
  Policy Studies at Victoria
  University of Wellington, 91
Institute of Welsh Affairs, 38
intergenerational equity, Earth
  Summit, Rio de Janeiro, 28
Intergovernmental Panel on
  Climate Change, 135
Intergovernmental Science-Policy
  Platform on Biodiversity and
  Ecosystem Services, 134
Irish Sea and dolphin counting,
  25–26

J
Jackson, Tim, on greatness in
  planning for future, 160–61
Jader, Layla, 24
Jenkins, Emily-Rose, 100
Jenkins, Victoria, 71, 75
Jervis, Ros, 120
Joint Parliamentary Committee
  for the Future (U.K.), 134
Jones, Carwyn
  Minister for Environment,
  Planning and Countryside,
  41, 60, 74, 77, 81, 82,
  153, 156
  on sustainability, 156–57
Joseph Rowntree Foundation, 16

Index

Juniper, Tony, *x*
justice. *See* environmental
justice; social justice

K
Kite Committee, 137
Kumar, Satish, on ecology and
economy, 141–43
Kyoto Protocol, 131

L
Labour Party
Foot, Michael, 14
Manifesto for 2011 general
election, 72
'The New Hope for Britain,'
14–15
in Wales, 5
land reclamation and Project
Skyline, 141, 145–51
language
Celtic, of Wales, 3–4
Urdd Gobaith Cymru, 83
Urdd National Eisteddfod,
4, 144
Welsh, and students, 84
learning, 20–22, 137–53
'Learning to Live Differently,'
32–38, 40, 50, 138
legislation, argument for, 74–77
legislative models, studies by
Andrea Ross, 75–76
Lewis, Huw (Minister for Commu-
nities and Tackling Poverty), 81
Liberal Democrats (Wales), 128

life expectancy in Wales, 5
Limits to Growth, The (Meadows),
19–21
*Limits to Growth: The 30-Year
Update* (Meadows), 20–21
Lincoln, Abraham, 125
Little Voices Making a
Difference, 123
'Living Wage' employees, 117, 124
'Llanelli We Want, The,' 84
Lleisiau Bach Little Voices
projects, 123
loving, 22
contributors from beyond
Wales, 166–69
optimism, 156
as a 'soft tool,' 20
tree planting, 155–56
voices of hope, 157–66
Lucas, Caroline, on Future
Generations Bill (U.K.), 167

M
M4 Relief Road, 116–17, 126
Mandela, Nelson, 27
Marshall, George, 96
Maslow's hierarchy of needs, 13
McGregor, Betsy, 136
McKenna, Mark, on equality,
162–63
Meadows, Donella, 25, 69, 103,
137, 143–44, 155, 171
Beyond the Limits, 20–21, 173
*Limits to Growth: The 30-Year
Update*, 19–21

Meadows, Donella (*continued*)
'soft tools' for sustainable
future, 20–22
Meikle, Anne, 95–96
mental models for future
thinking, 173
MHP Communications, 100
Middleton, Andy, 51, 54–55, 97
Millennium Development Goals
(MDGs) (UN), 44, 83
Miller, Nick, 102
Miller, Vashti, 100–101
mining industry, 4–5, 14
Morgan, Rhodri, 15–16, 40, 46, 52
'One Wales, One Planet,' 54–55
'Yes for Wales,' 65–66
Morgan, Shan (Permanent
Secretary), 107–8
Morrison, Scott (PM, Australia),
105
Morrow, Karen, 22
Muhith, Justina, on employment,
165–66

N
National Assembly for Wales, 3,
17, 26, 29–38, 46–48, 76, 82
Auditor General for Wales,
113–14
commitment to the Act,
127–28
review, five-year, of the
Act, 113
and sustainable development,
127

Sustainable Development
Scheme, 188–89
The Well-being of Future
Generations (Wales) Act,
89–92
'National Assembly for Wales and
Taking the Longer View, The'
(Roderick), 76
National Eisteddfod of Wales,
4, 144
National Forest, new, 121
National Local Government
Forum Against Poverty, 16
National Museum Wales and
biodiversity, 121
National Waterfront Museum, 121
National Wool Museum, 121
nature's rights, 140
Netherwood, Alan, 39, 61–62, 96
Netherwood Sustainable
Futures, 96
networking, 20, 21
New Green Deal, 163, 164
'New Hope for Britain, The,'
14–15
North Wales Wildlife Trust, 31

O
Older People's Commissioner, 92
One Planet Developments (OPDs),
14, 18, 46–50, 115–16, 148
reconnecting with the
land, 18
'One Planet Wales' (Parry), 48,
49, 50, 143

Index

'One Wales, One Planet'
Effectiveness Review by
PwC, 78
launching of, 54–55
text of, 56–58, 181–85
third scheme of the Act, 50–58
One Young World, 99, 100
OPDs. *See* One Planet
Developments
O'Riordan, Tim, x
Our Common Future (World
Commission on Environment
and Development), 33
outdoor learning, 43–44, 121
Oxfam, 73
Oxford Junior Dictionary
and words for natural
phenomenon, 70

P
Palmer, Michael, 68
Parry, Morgan, 48, 141
lecture to Urdd National
Eisteddfod, 143–45
Passivhaus standards for
housing, 119
Paull, Laline, *The Bees and
the Ice*, 169
Pembrokeshire Coast Path,
12–13, 69–70
Permanent Secretary's role in the
Act, 128
place-making, 116, 176
Plaid Cymru (The Party of
Wales), 47, 50, 128

plastic bags, reducing use of,
48, 63–64
Porritt, Jonathon, 42, 140–41
poverty, 5
The Big Issue magazine, 133
National Local Government
Forum Against Poverty, 16
statistics on, 16
Pritchard, Sue, 92, 118
Private Finance Initiative
(PFI), 132
Programme for Government
shift in governance in Wales,
77–79
sustainability legislation, 74
Project Skyline, 141, 145–51
'Proposals for a Sustainable
Development Bill,' 79–81
prosperity, new definition of,
91, 132
public buildings and alternative
energy, 41
Public Health Wales, 120
Public Services Boards, 82–83,
86, 109, 140
PwC (PricewaterhouseCoopers),
78

Q
Quinn, Matthew, 73

R
Rawindaran, Nisha, 136
recycling and reusing
achievements, 124

recycling and reusing (*continued*)
  plastic bags, reducing use of,
    48, 63–64
  public sector refurbishment,
    120–21
  targets, 18, 63, 135
  'Towards Zero Waste,' 63, 98
  zero-waste efforts, 100,
    168–69
refurbishment in public sector, 120
Regenerating Our City for
  Well-being and Wildlife
  (Swansea), 121
renewables, as part of second
  scheme, 41
Rhodesian Front government, 11
Ricketts, Becky, 99
'Right to Food,' 168
Riversimple and hydrogen car
  manufacturing, 118
Roderick, Peter, 'The National
  Assembly for Wales and Taking
  the Longer View,' 76
Roscoe, Chris, 99
Ross, Andrea, 75
Royal Society for the Protection
  of Birds (RSPB), 15, 30, 31

S
St Fagans National Museum of
  History, 121
Sargeant, Carl (Minister for
  Natural Resources), 1, 87–88
schemes. *See* Sustainable
  Development Schemes

school meals, sustainable, 42, 59
Schumacher College, 142
Senedd Cymru, 152
Seth, Nikhil, 1
  well-being goals, seven, 112–13
Seymour, John, 13–14
Sharp, Leith, 154, 157–58
Sheen, Michael, and Unicef U.K.,
  84, 157–58
Sheers, Owen, 'Term,' 158–59
Smit, Tim, *x*
Smith, Fern, on the future, 166–67
social justice, 5, 81–83
  increasing, in Wales, 152–53
  Leith Sharp on, 157–58
soft tools for sustainable future,
  20–22, 144
solar energy, 118
Stagecoach and electric buses, 119
'Starting to Live Differently,' 138
Stockholm Environment Institute
  at the University of York, 50
Stockley, Joe, 99–100
Sustain, 168
sustainable development
  Agenda 21 of Earth Summit,
    1992, 19
  as central organizing
    principle, 65–66
  changing standards of, 76–77
  defined in paper by Bates,
    56–58
  developing laws for, 22–23
  effects of the Act, 114–15
  increasing, in Wales, 152–53

Index

Labour Party manifesto,
66–67
The Limits to Growth (Meadows), 19–21
U.K. policy in 1990s, 27–29
Sustainable Development Alliance, 73, 81, 87–88
Sustainable Development and Business Decision Making in the Welsh Assembly Government (Wales Audit Office), 58–60
Sustainable Development Bill, 82
Sustainable Development Charter, 61, 78
Sustainable Development Commission (SDC), 29, 34, 42, 64, 70
Sustainable Development Coordinators Cymru, 59–60
Sustainable Development Goals (SDGs), 83, 134
Sustainable Development Scheme of the National Assembly for Wales, 188–89
Sustainable Development Schemes, 7
'Learning to Live Differently,' 32–38
'One Wales, One Planet,' 46–58
'Starting to Live Differently,' 38–46
Sustainable Development Strategy (U.K.), 28–29
Sustainable Futures Commissioner, 64, 88–89

Swansea Bay Tidal Lagoon, 118
Swansea's green infrastructure, 121

T
Tŷ Pawb covered market, 114–15
term limits for Welsh politicians, 66, 72
'Term' (Sheers), 158–59
Thatcher, Margaret, 14
Thomas, Rhodri, 98
Thoreau, Henry David, 9, 13
Thorpe, David, 102
Thunberg, Greta, 1, 105
tidal power, 118
'Towards Zero Waste,' 63, 98
town center regeneration, 114
Townsend, Solitaire, 102
Tram, Dan, 100
transport
Cardiff Airport, 126
clean air and public health, 119
electric vehicles for public fleet, 119
hydrogen car manufacturing, 118
M4 Relief Road, 116–17
Stagecoach and electric buses, 119
Transport for Wales and Metro plans, 118
tree planting
Davidson's land, 155–56
National Forest project, 121

#futuregen

Treherbert and Project
Skyline, 148
truth-telling, 21
accountability and the Act,
103–35
review of the Act, 110–14
as a 'soft tool,' 20
town center regeneration, 114
Tully, Catarina, 8
Tutu, Archbishop Desmond, 3

U
UN Convention on Biological
Diversity, 88
UN Convention on the Rights of
the Child, 123
UN Global Goals, 1
unions and mining strike,
1984, 14
University of South Wales, 100
University of Wales Trinity Saint
David, 99
Upadhyaya, Meena, on
multicultural society and
education, 166
Urdd Gobaith Cymru, 83–84
Urdd National Eisteddfod, 4
lecture by Morgan Parry,
143–45

V
visioning
for first scheme, 33–34
for 'One Wales, One Planet,' 53
as a 'soft tool,' 20–21

W
Wales
Celtic language, 3–4
cultural celebrations, 4
geography of, 4
Industrial Revolution, 4–5, 130
life expectancy, 5
natural resources of, 4–6,
12–13
resources used for industry,
4–5
tourism, 4
Wales Audit Office, 113
*Sustainable Development and
Business Decision Making
in the Welsh Assembly
Government*, 58–60
'Wales Carers Want, The,' 84
Wales Council for Voluntary
Action, 99–100
Wales Environment Link, 35
'Wales for Africa' fair trade
initiative, 44–45, 59
Wales Sustainability Forum
(Cynnal Cymru), 34
Wales We Want, The,' 83–89
'Wales We Want in 2050, The,' 152
'Wales We Want Report: A Report
on Behalf of Future Genera-
tions, The,' 85–86
'Wales Women Want, The,' 84
'Wales Young Farmers Want,
The,' 84
waste management. *See* recycling
and reusing

Index

well-being goals, seven, 112–13
well-being objectives, achieving, 110
Well-being of Future Generations (Wales) Act, The, 88–92
    contributions to governance, 122–35
    effects across different sectors, 114–21
    general election, 129
    global inspiration of, 131–32
    Government of Wales Act 1998, 31
    influence of Rhodesia on, 9–14
    leadership, 139
    prosperity, redefining of, 91
    provisions, selected list of, 89–90
    seven well-being goals, 112–13
    as 'soft power,' 6
    support and financial mechanisms for, 140
    three limbs, draft of, 1–3, 76
    'well-being goals,' 89
Welsh Climate Change Commission, 47, 50, 53
Welsh Labour, 66–67, 128
Welsh-language Commissioner, 92
Welsh Local Government Association, 16–17
Welsh Youth Forum for Sustainable Development (WYFSD), 37
Welsh Youth Parliament, 37, 100, 122

Wickremasinghe, Mishan, 100
wildlife. *See also* biodiversity
    in Africa, 10
    dolphin count, 25–26
    Kite Committee, 137
    Lleisiau Bach / Little Voices, 123
    National Museum Wales and, 121
    outdoor education, 147–48
    Pembrokeshire Coast Path, 69–70
    rights of nature, 140–41
    Swansea renewal plans, 118, 121
Wildlife Trusts, 80
Williams, Catriona, 24
Williams, Eifion, 98
Williams, Iolo, on nature and outdoors education, 160–61
Wilson, Julie, 24
wind power and local communities, 5–6
woodlands and Project Skyline, 147–48
World Commission on Environment and Development, *Our Common Future*, 33
World Future Council, 5
'World We Want, The,' 83
World Wildlife Fund (WWF), 34, 39, 73, 80–81, 87
    'Progress of Embedding the 'One Planet' Aspiration in Welsh Government,' 61–62

World Wildlife Fund (*continued*)
'One Planet Wales,' 48
Sustainable Development
Alliance, 81
WWF Cymru, 48, 95, 141, 143
Wright, Simon, 138

Y
'Yes for Wales' campaign, 66
Young Leaders Academy, 122
Youth Forum for Sustainable
Development, 122

Youth Parliament, 37, 122
youth, participation of
Children as Researchers, 123
Funky Dragon, 122
Lleisiau Bach / Little
Voices, 123
United Nations Convention on
the Rights of the Child, 123
voices on the Act, 99–101

Z
zero-waste efforts, 100, 168–69

ABOUT THE AUTHOR

Aled Llywelyn

Jane Davidson is the Pro Vice-Chancellor Emeritus at the University of Wales Trinity Saint David. From 2000–2011, she was Minister for Education, then Minister for Environment, Sustainability and Housing in the Welsh Government where she proposed legislation to make sustainable development its central organising principle; the Well-being of Future Generations (Wales) Act came into law in April 2015. She introduced the first plastic bag charge in the UK, and her recycling regulations took Wales to third best in the world. She created the Climate Change Commission for Wales, the post of Sustainable Futures Commissioner and the Wales Coast Path. In education, she piloted major curriculum changes for early years – the Foundation Phase, the Welsh Baccalaureate and integrated Education for Sustainable Development and Global Citizenship – into the Welsh curriculum. Jane is a patron of the Chartered Institute for Ecology and Environmental Management (CIEEM) and Tools for Self Reliance (TFSR Cymru). She holds honorary fellowships from WWF, Chartered Institution of Wastes Management, Chartered Institution of Water and Environmental Management. Jane is chair of the RSA in Wales and in 2017 was guest faculty in the Executive Education for Sustainability Leadership programme at Harvard University's T.H. Chan School of Public Health. She lives on a smallholding in West Wales where she aims to live lightly on the land.

Young Voices

From the 'One Young World' conference in London 2019

What would they change in their countries if they had a Well-being of Future Generations Act?

Policies which allow for youths to be able to speak for themselves on any matters that affect their lives; the ability to hold governments accountable.

PIERRE, 19, Caribbean

Include a percentage of parliamentary seats for young people so they can represent the voice of youths.

AHMED, 28, Egypt

Every child, regardless of their gender and background, should have access to mandatory 12 years of basic education.

OLUWAFUNMILAYO, 24, Nigeria

Introduce a social tax for corporate organisations to ensure or safeguard the consumers from ridiculous profits they make, and the government to channel the funds into welfare. Eighty per cent of GDP to go directly to health care, along with laws which bridge the gap in the inequality in the health care system in South Africa.

ABIGAIL, 28, South Africa

Amend the law that restricts young people from running for political office in Seychelles.

ANAEL, 27, Seychelles

Young Voices

Government should create access to clean and affordable energy for everyone.

SALOME, 26, Zimbabwe

Government should provide 18 years' mandatory education. Policies to engage women to 50 per cent levels in all sectors.

AYAN, 26, Somaliland

Set presidential term limits to 5 years maximum and not more than 10 years in office per electorate.

MBYIDZENYUY, 30, Cameroon

Create laws to enable the LGBTQ+ community to adopt or to enable them to have offsprings.

FEDERICO, 29, Switzerland

Effective implementation of the constitution, regulation and policies. Totally free secondary and tertiary education across the country.

TRESOR, 27, Congo-Kinshasa

Allow for free speech from citizens.

NEVYL, 27, Congo-Brazzaville

If I could change something in my country it would be the tax because our tax is just too damn high.

ALVARO, 25, Philippines

The law that I would like to change back is that the president said that any woman, girl, who got pregnant during her secondary education could not go back to her secondary education after having the child, and I just think that that is unfair because in some circumstances it wasn't her choice to be necessarily when she would get pregnant or when she would have the child, so if you want to solve the problem, maybe just put her back in school after, thank you.

ANONYMOUS, 21, Tanzania

Young Voices

Women's rights, especially in divorce cases as it stands right now, because women cannot get a divorce by themselves, and even where they can, they get dragged into courts for years and years and years.

AMEENA, 27, Bahrain

I would cancel the law that is purely discriminatory, the anti-LGBT one – it's called Propaganda of Homosexuality – which basically bans any mentions in the media, and people can basically get arrested for expressing anything, like in protest. It could be really widely interpreted and used wherever the legislatives would like when they enforce it, and by itself it's just basically pure homophobia.

ANONYMOUS, 29, Russia

There is one particular [law] that has bothered me in Malaysia: child marriage. There's no actual law to set the age the child can actually get married, so a law like this would prevent child marriage and would allow all female students to actually pursue education, so they don't get married and be confined in households.

ASHIWIN, 29, Malaysia

If I had to overturn one law, it would be the executive orders that Trump has implemented affecting immigration. The United States is a land that is accepting of everyone regardless of the nation they come from, the religion they have, their beliefs, and through his executive orders, it's creating a divide in the nation and ultimately widespread hatred.

DEREK, 25, United States

I would make all education inclusive of LGBTQ+ relationships and people. I think we are at a stage where young people are not taught about different groups, which means it's easier for them to grow up with fear and hate; whereas, actually if we taught people about different groups earlier, we know that people's hearts grow with love and accepting. And I would rather see that from the outset than wait for things to get worse.

LAUREN, 27, U.K.

Young Voices

I would love to change a lot of laws, but in order for those laws to be changed in my country, we'd need more women in power. So for me the first step is to get more women in power, because with that they would be able to influence policies that affect the lives of girls in every part of the country – so laws that make sure that sex offenders get into jail, laws that make sure that girls have access to sanitary towels, have access to education and any other basic needs.

MARY, 25, Uganda

A treaty to recognise the rights of the aboriginal people.

ELISSA, 25, Australia

Northern Nigeria has a system where essentially you have child marriage of teenagers or early teens, who often marry elders and senior men, and I think that law obviously needs to be fundamentally changed No young lady should be getting married before, in my opinion, at least 18 or 21. Thanks.

KOJO, 26, Nigeria

One policy I would like the government to change is to promote more youths to get into farming – provide grants, schemes, assistance – for the new generation to embrace farming.

RNESH, 26, Fiji Islands

What I would change is legislation in the Netherlands for young people – for starters on the house market, so that they are able to buy a house for the future.

ROELAND, Netherlands

The one piece of legislation that I would change in Jamaica is making education free for everyone, because I believe that the foundation of a community or a country is educating the population and making sure that they are able to contribute to the country and to its betterment.

JAMES, 23, Jamaica

Young Voices

For us to be able to freely protest, campaign for anything, without having to get permission.

FIONA, 26, Singapore

What we are fighting for in Hong Kong right now is universal suffrage, basically having the freedom for everyone to select our leader in Hong Kong.

KIM, 23, Hong Kong

My reform would be around justice, actually, because if we can get the justice system in Nigeria right, everything else would fall in place. The justice system cannot currently hold the government to account for anything, because the government runs the justice system, so if we can get that right then I feel like everyone else will behave themselves.

TOBI, 28, Nigeria

If we had a quota of water for every household – for example, in London, say if on average a household uses X cubic metres of water every year, we say OK you can have this plus 10 or 20 per cent to be conservative and every cubic metre of water you use in addition you pay 5 or 10 times the price.

VIVIEN, 29, France

The one thing I would like to change in my country is that I would love to have more freedom of speech or freedom of media because right now it is still very, quite, difficult and dangerous for us to freely express what we think about politics and our point of views on the government et cetera.

ANONYMOUS, 25, Vietnam

In my opinion, in the future, I would like to see that more people in China have easier access to policy making and things like that so we can actually do more for ourselves and our society instead of just waiting for someone else to do it.

CUI, 28, China